WHITE PRIVILEGE

WHITE PRIVILEGE

GEORGES GUISCARD

ARKTOS
LONDON 2025

ΛRKTOS

⊕ Arktos.com 𝐟 fb.com/Arktos ◐ ⊙ arktosmedia ✖ arktosjournal

Le privilège blanc: Qui veut faire la peau aux Européens?, published as part of the *Collection Iliade* by La Nouvelle Librairie éditions in 2021.

ISBN
978-1-917646-94-9 (Paperback)
978-1-917646-95-6 (Hardback)
978-1-917646-96-3 (Ebook)

Translation
Roger Adwan

Editing
Jafe Arnold

Layout and Cover
Tor Westman

CONTENTS

❦

PREFACE

ALTHOUGH THE author does indeed attempt to limit his remarks to the concept of white privilege, it is impossible to address this issue without having to mention other notions as well, sometimes even at length.

Whiteness, de-colonisation, patriarchy, cultural appropriation, micro-aggressions, unconscious racism, critical race theory,[1] intersectionality,[2] Black studies... It is impossible to be exhaustive, as the list seems to be growing on a daily basis. This avalanche of disciplines or elements of language, intended to crush the opponent with a succession of pseudo-scientific terms that are all, in fact, arguments of authority, cannot be ignored.

We thus ask our readers to kindly tolerate the use of the terms and typical jargon employed by those that criticise alleged white privilege. Please also be aware of the fact that, despite the debatable nature of many of these theories, the author has decided not to use quotation marks or '(sic)' in order not to burden the text unnecessarily. Please be assured that these concepts will be mentioned as little as possible, and always with the aim of presenting the subject of this book, namely white privilege, more effectively.

---

1   Translator's Note [TN]: Critical race theory (CRT) is an academic discipline established by law professors who use blatantly Marxist analysis to conclude that racial dominance by Whites has created what they term 'systemic racism'.

2   TN: Intersectionality is defined as an analytical framework that focuses on how various aspects of a person's social and political position allegedly come together to create unique experiences of both discrimination and privilege.

Furthermore, the term 'West' will surface frequently through-out this book. This, however, should not be seen as some kind of ideological consideration. Indeed, critics of white privilege simply conflate the latter indistinguishably with the West, understood as meaning the white world in general. To them, no distinction is to be made between a European from the Old Continent, a white person from Montana, and a Boer from South Africa. Since we all know, thanks to Julien Freund, that 'it is your enemy that designates you', we have chosen to accept this designation, which reflects a transfor-mation of political representations within the countries of European civilisation.

DOWN WITH THE WHITE MAN!

'*Being a white man can be experienced as a privilege*'. These words are not those of some obscure left-wing activist of African descent. Indeed, it was none other than Emmanuel Macron himself who echoed the theory of white privilege in an interview with *L'Express* on 22 December 2020. Our head of state 'noted that, in our society, being white creates objectively easier conditions to access the position that is [one's] own, find housing and be given a job, compared to being an Asian, black, or North African man, or an Asian, black, or North African woman.'

Having long remained clandestine in France, the idea that white privilege actually exists burst into public debate in mid-2020. Following the death of African-American repeat offender George Floyd, large-scale demonstrations initially shook the United States alone. The demonstrations of the American 'Black Lives Matter' movement, in which people protested against allegedly widespread racist police violence, then resonated in France as well, serving as a pretext for the Adama Committee (named after French-Malian offender Adama Traoré, who was also a convicted felon and died after attempting to escape police custody) to organise several rallies centred around the same issue in France.

The concept of white privilege was notably taken up by novelist Virginie Despentes after her participation in one of these demonstrations: *'Privilege is having the choice to either think about it, or not [...] I can forget that I'm white'*. These remarks caused quite a sensation. Several major media outlets, including *Le Parisien*, *Libération*, and *France Culture*, rushed to clarify them, only too happy to be able to support the Traoré gang and make white people feel guilty. Since then, white privilege has been present everywhere.

It took a mere six months and a few demonstrations organised by activist groups that have been infiltrated by both the decolonial movement and Islamism for a theory originating from the American radical left to be presented by the French president as a fact structuring our European societies. Having become unavoidable, supposed white privilege is now exploited in a thousand ways to demonise Europeans. In all Western countries, it is increasingly hurled as an insult in the face of white people, all of whom are deemed guilty of enjoying an unfair structural advantage.

The entire discourse on white privilege can be summed up in a few words: European societies are structured around a white norm, to the point that its beneficiaries are unaware of it. So, white people have actually created societies in their own image? One might be inclined to wonder where the issue is...

I

GENEALOGY OF
THE CONCEPT

Notions Derived from Marxism

THE CONCEPT of white privilege was developed in 1975 by American communist activist Theodore W. Allen. In the context of the Civil Rights Movement aimed at abolishing segregation in the United States, he proceeded to write, beginning in 1965, various articles exploring the concepts of white supremacy and the white race, all within an anti-capitalist approach to the labour movement.

Working with historian Noel Ignatiev, also a communist activist who later called for the '*abolition of the white race*', Allen developed the idea of a 'white blind spot', which refers to an inability to perceive the social advantages of belonging to the white majority and dominant white population. In his first book, *Class Struggle and the Origin of Racial Slavery: The Invention of the White Race*, published in 1975, he traces back the idea of an 'invented' white race (as a socio-racial category) to late 17th-century American colonial plantations, in order to hierarchise and divide workers by bestowing 'white privilege' on some.

Allen was inspired by sociologist William Edward Burghardt Du Bois, an African-American scholar who wrote in 1935:

It must be remembered that the white group of laborers, while they received a low wage, were compensated in part by a sort of public and
psychological wage. They were given public deference and titles of cour-
tesy because they were white. They were admitted freely with all classes
of white people to public functions, public parks, and the best schools.
The police were drawn from their ranks, and the courts, dependent upon
their votes, treated them with such leniency as to encourage lawlessness.
[...] White labor saw in every advance of Negroes a threat to their racial
prerogatives.

Just as Theodore W. Allen's political affinities suggest, the embry-
onic concept of white privilege is underpinned by notions derived
from Marxism. Historically, the latter presents itself as a method
of analysing history scientifically through an economic lens. While
some Marxist analyses have proven relevant, including, for instance,
the downward pressure on wages resulting from immigration and
Gramsci's cultural hegemony, the historical perspectives developed by
Marx have actually proven false.

Karl Marx and Friedrich Engels theorised the coming end of the
capitalist system, which served the interests of the dominant class,
and its replacement with socialism through a revolution conducted
by the exploited. Socialism was thus seen as an intermediate stage
during which people would prepare for the advent of an egalitarian,
classless communist society free of any and all individual ownership
of the means of production, without a state, and comprising socially
equal people freed from the alienation of working for the sake of
survival. In Marx's time, meaning the mid- and late-19th century, the
dominant ones were to be found within the propertied capitalist class
embodied by the bourgeoisie. As for the exploited, they were none
other than property-less proletarian workers.

Despite the various, unsuccessful, and often bloody attempts to
implement this vision, it is all too clear that the anticipated revolution does not seem likely to arise. And yet, this Manichaean dichot-
omy still permeates the left-wing mentality, to which this approach

remains essentially relevant. Indeed, it retains the status of a prophecy to be fulfilled, as the oppressed always wage a struggle against their oppressors, although, of course, the theory has had to be adjusted to reflect contemporary realities.

The evolution of these ideas, whose later offshoots do not always acknowledge their undeniably objective genealogy, is easily traceable. To outline things in broad terms, it begins with critical theory, a Marxist philosophical line of thought developed during the 1930s in Germany by the Frankfurt School of Theodor Adorno and Max Horkheimer, whose sociological approach aims to identify and challenge societal and cultural 'structures', i.e. the power relations that structure societies. In Horkheimer's words, the objective is to '*liberate people from the circumstances that enslave them*'.

These concerns ended up fuelling postmodern philosophy. The poststructuralists of what was called 'French Theory' in the United States ('deconstructionists' such as Michel Foucault, Simone de Beauvoir, Gilles Deleuze, and Jacques Derrida, all of whom were adepts of integral relativism, of questioning all meaning and all legitimacy) retained various axioms and schemata of critical theory, including an emphasis on structures of domination. To Foucault, every norm is synonymous with oppression, everything a 'prison'. While, during the 1960s, these precursors were mostly French, their successors in the 1970s were mostly American. The influence of this postmodern and de-constructivist approach subsequently surfaced in academic disciplines that largely pertain to militancy and pseudoscience, such as gender studies and post-colonialism.

Race and Domination

The introduction of such ideas onto American campuses, which have always been more preoccupied with racial issues than those of the Old Continent, led in the mid-1980s to the latest major embodiment of such analyses with a focus on power relations: critical race theory. With its vague ideological corpus, this school is above all a prism of militant interpretations; and it is partly this flexibility that allows it today to occupy a hegemonic position in the Anglo-Saxon academic world, thus enabling it to gain ground throughout the Western world. Critical race theory combines modern racial issues with the critical theory of the Frankfurt School, as well as with postmodern deconstructionist tendencies. The basic premise is that, being the group that holds the reigns of power, whites exercise *de facto* a protean sort of domination — whether political, economic, cultural, symbolic or any other — over non-whites, all of whom are kept in a state of subjugation.

Hiding behind wordy theories and concepts, this shift is easy to summarise when reduced to its simplest expression. While maintaining the binary Marxist scheme of dominant versus dominated, it is whites that have replaced the bourgeoisie, with minorities acting as the new oppressed proletariat.

Despite spanning several decades within the history of ideas, such a shift from class to race is, in fact, natural. According to Marx, group identities or rationales are those that establish power. Following in his footsteps and influenced by the Frankfurt School, Foucault[1] considers power relations to be the root of all domination and hierarchies through a twofold play of social control and oppression. Last but not least, we have Pierre Bourdieu,[2] who was labelled a 'major mishap in French thought' and an 'intellectual Chernobyl that never ceases to irradiate us' by François Bousquet.[3] In the 1970s, he both criticised and developed Marxism by replacing the economic and social violence of class struggle with a rather difficult-to-grasp concept of 'symbolic violence' perpetrated by the dominant ones, who impose their own norms upon the dominated.

---

1   TN: While also active as an author, literary critic, political activist, and teacher, Paul-Michel Foucault was a French 'historian of ideas' and philosopher.

2   TN: Pierre Bourdieu was a French sociologist and public intellectual whose work was primarily focused on the dynamics of power in society.

3   TN : François Bousquet is a French journalist, essayist and editor.

According to Bourdieu, these norms act *'as the imposition of cultural arbitrariness at the hands of an arbitrary power'*. Symbolic violence represents a struggle that is no longer class-based and vertical, but rather horizontalised into group struggle. The cultural domination of certain groups supports their social domination by fostering the internalisation of hierarchies and norms among those subjected to it, both of which are, likewise, the product of dominant groups.

For the proponents of critical race theory, this domination is embodied in modern America by the perpetuation of what they consider to be white supremacy, a supremacy that stems from the American colonial and slavery system. Just as it favoured whites over black slaves at the time, widespread racism now favours whites over various racial minorities. It didn't take long for this pattern to be transposed word for word to Europe, a continent that is considered guilty of having colonised the entire world and, thereby, of having created the same racist structures as the slave-owning United States.

This applies even to Western countries that never actually had colonies, because it is whites as a whole that have been charged with inventing racism and the hierarchy of races and with having generally benefited from them. This is one of the grievances now levelled at whites: prior to white colonialism, there may have been some xenophobia, bloody wars, invasions and territory occupations, or even large-scale slavery. But at the time, peoples did not allegedly think of themselves in racial terms or in accordance with a hierarchy of superiority and inferiority. By colonising the entire planet and imposing their cultural model as a reference, white people are alleged to have spread this infamous racism, which is both hierarchical and dehumanising.

The Ubiquity of Privilege

It is hardly surprising that these ideas originated in the United States, since the country's history was marked by slavery and, until the 1960s, by racial segregation. Critical race theory is rooted in a school of legal thought according to which discrimination did not disappear with the Civil Rights Act of 1964, which abolished the above-mentioned segregation. In the eyes of its founders, including Richard Delgado, who also campaigned in favour of a ban on genetic or cognitive research related to human populations, and Derrick Bell, discrimination remains *de facto* deeply rooted in American society, even if American law did put an end to *de jure* discrimination.

When not enshrined in law, discrimination is purportedly maintained through prejudice and stereotypes, thus perpetuating social inequalities that would otherwise be completely unjustified: greater poverty among ethnic minorities, ghettos, difficulties in finding housing or a job, racial profiling and trigger-happy police officers. Because privileged groups — the wealthy, men, and whites — are alleged to have historically held more power within society, they could continue to impose their codes and norms, to which disadvantaged groups would have ever greater difficulty conforming. A vicious circle is thus allegedly perpetuated, since the status collectively enjoyed by the privileged would *ipso facto* and unconsciously push the latter to try and maintain it.

From such a perspective, the racism that individuals experience no longer requires any concrete, deliberate, or blatant discrimination. It is, instead, alleged to exist at a level encompassing entire Western nations, since these were shaped by whites and are based on their norms. This 'white privilege' is so deeply embedded in the West that, in effect, all whites, regardless of their individual social status, benefit from a structural advantage inherent in our societies.

In this respect, white countries are purported to constantly favour whites in one way or another and, in fact, to permanently harm ethnic groups that do not naturally fit the canons of whiteness. White privilege does not imply systematic success, but rather fewer difficulties for whites than for others: regardless of his/her personal situation, a white person supposedly always benefits, at the very least, from the absence of the negative consequences that stem from omnipresent racism, while also remaining indifferent to the suffering of others.

In more specific terms, a homeless white person is somehow still more privileged than a black or Arab person in the same situation. They are even alleged to be, in some ways, always more privileged than a socially well-integrated black person, as the latter could more readily lose their status, while a homeless white person could escape their situation more easily. In all cases, moreover, non-white people are said to remain victims of racism on a daily basis... even when they have never had to complain of any discrimination or derogatory remarks!

This so-called systemic or institutional racism is even said to be so structuring, so diffuse, and so internalised that one is most often subjected to it without the necessity of any real discrimination taking place and regardless of whether the victim is aware of it or not. Racism is allegedly experienced on a daily basis, with a constant focus on the races or native cultures of the minorities in question: a group of North Africans wearing jogging pants that see a white woman cross to the other side of the street; an African man being asked if he's a good dancer; a fully veiled Muslim woman that people gaze at with astonishment... If a white person is refused an apartment rental, they will never ask themselves if it was due to their skin colour, whereas a North African will most likely wonder. Privilege on the one hand, a mental burden and social suffering on the other.

It doesn't matter that many non-whites can live perfectly normal lives in the West without feeling discriminated against, sometimes even attaining very enviable positions. Whether they are ministers, company owners or famous TV presenters, they have inevitably had more difficulties in their careers than their privileged white counterparts: even if they never realised this; even if they have never had anything to complain about; and even if they emphatically deny this. They simply are victims, and that's all there is to it.

Several proponents of critical race theory even believe that some non-Whites have had to conform so thoroughly to the whiteness structuring our societies that, in order to succeed, they have become traitors. We are all familiar, for instance, with the humiliating terms 'Bounty' and 'house Negro' used to describe black people who have become police officers and serve the white State, a state which is deemed racist. According to these radical detractors of white privilege, whiteness is allegedly fluid and can be the attribute of non-Whites who have fully assimilated and succeeded: one can thus become white by assimilating, working hard at school, or creating one's own start-up! This socio-racial fluidity, however, remains a one-way street, as white people, *all* white people, remain structurally privileged.

In an article published in October 2020 in the weekly magazine *Marianne*, political scientist Pierre-André Taguieff explains that the terms 'institutional', 'structural' and 'systemic' racism originated in revolutionary African-American circles in the late 1960s. Re-defining racism through an activist interpretation, these notions, according to Taguieff, only serve as a *'symbolic weapon that consists in reducing racism to the white kind, which is supposedly inherent in "white society" or "white domination", with the latter being the only form of racial domination recognised and denounced by neo-anti-racists.'* White societies, 'essentialised and demonised as racist', are granted the attribute of racism, thus exculpating all other forms that the latter can take on, including, above all, anti-white racism. Simultaneously, white people and the West become the 'main focus of boundless hatred'.

THE AMPLIFIER OF INTERSECTIONAL FEMINISM

Dissemination of the Concept

THE CONCEPT of 'white privilege' had been restricted to private use until its popularisation in 1988 by American feminist and anti-racist activist Peggy McIntosh. Her article "White Privilege: Unpacking the Invisible Knapsack" listed 26 personally experienced examples of what she identified as everyday advantages linked to her skin colour — advantages that non-white people did not allegedly enjoy.

From '*I can be pretty sure that if I ask to talk to "the person in charge", I will be facing a person of my race*' to '*I can choose blemish cover or bandages in "flesh" colour and have them more less match my skin*', an example taken up at a much later time in France by Afro-feminist activist Rokhaya Diallo, the situations described to illustrate white privilege are intentionally banal. This is what would later come to be termed 'micro-aggressions': the idea that trivial and innocuous anecdotes that white people might even fail to notice can actually constitute a disadvantage, a source of discomfort or humiliation to non-whites.

Faced with this list, one almost smiles with frustration upon reading about the white privilege felt by Peggy McIntosh when, in 1988, she was able to '*go shopping alone most of the time, pretty well assured that [she would] not be followed or harassed*'; or how she was never asked to '*speak for all the people of [her] racial group.*' How things have changed since then!

Peggy McIntosh's article caused quite a stir in American universities, giving rise to an entire academic movement known as *whiteness studies*. Summed up by McIntosh herself, the idea is as follows: she had been '*taught to see racism only in individual acts of meanness*' before realising that it actually lay '*in invisible systems conferring dominance on [her] group*'. By means of that text, her goal was to drive white people out of a certain type of denial. This was so successfully achieved that the idea of white privilege has prevailed both on campuses across the Atlantic and within the Western activist left.

This echoes Theodore W. Allen's idea of a white blind spot. According to McIntosh, it prevents white people from understanding that they have organised their societies according to a 'white norm', centring them around whiteness. This white privilege, which is a constituent of our social relations and an integral part of our Western societies, is so natural that it becomes invisible to those that benefit from it. In order to destroy this system, one must expose it, and make white people aware of their own 'blind spot', of their white privilege[1], so that they can think of themselves in 'racial terms'.

McIntosh's short text was actually excerpted from a longer one published shortly before, in which the feminist author analyses more broadly the links between white privilege and male privilege.

Feminism Takes On Male Privilege

Third-wave feminism was indeed the perfect accelerator, a fertile breeding ground coupled with a vast capacity for resonance within universities and, more generally, among the female population. In the aftermath of such topics as the legal status of women, their right

---

1   TN: McIntosh actually labels the term 'privilege' as 'misleading', because to her, 'the conditions [...] work systematically to overempower certain groups.'

to vote, and their right to work, all of which were raised between the mid-19th and mid-20th century, in addition to further issues such as sexual liberation and the right to abortion, which remained current until the 1970s, the feminist movement found itself without a worthy aim to struggle for.

Since the 1980s and 1990s, feminism, now imbued with *queer* theory (a term meaning 'bizarre' or 'strange' and encompassing all sexualities or behaviours that diverge from traditional heterosexuality) has expanded its scope of action. In the name of the fight against patriarchy and male privilege, it has been acting as a travelling companion to other struggles connected with marginal sexualities, as the world witnesses the trivialisation of LGBT movements, gender ideology, racial and religious minorities, physical and mental disabilities, obesity, and so on. And all the latter are alleged to be groups that patriarchal society and toxic masculinity oppress in one way or another.

One might wonder about the priorities espoused by these feminists, who, for example, remained silent when hundreds of women were sexually assaulted by hordes of North Africans on New Year's Eve 2016 in Cologne, as acknowledged by German police. In their eyes, this topic is secondary to the use of an inclusive grammar, one which would not diminish the position and place of women: in French, for instance, they would want to introduce such words as '*celleux*' instead of '*ceux*' or '*les ami-e-s*'[2] so as to to fight against male

---

2   TN: To give English readers an idea of what those feminists are campaigning for, it is all rather similar to the 'English' use of so-called neo-pronouns such as 'ze/hir', 'xe/xyr', and other nonsense — the difference being that whereas in English, plural personal pronouns, demonstratives, possessives, etc. tend to be gender neutral ('they', 'those', 'their', etc.), the French language makes clear distinctions between the feminine and the masculine. 'Those', for instance, is translated as *ceux* for the masculine and *celles* for the feminine. Even plural nouns differ in French: *amis* for male friends and *amies* for female friends. In cases where both genders are represented, the masculine form is applied. Those 'feminists', however, are now calling for the combination of such words into one, resulting in gibberish like '*celleux*' or '*ami-e-s*'.

privilege and signal the presence of at least one woman in a given group. It must be said that, not being white, North Africans also form an oppressed category. It is therefore difficult to blame them for anything.

Such considerations are ultimately no more delusional than the actual intellectual figures of the movement itself. One obviously thinks of Judith Butler, the 'popess' of feminism, who is unanimously celebrated for a work that is ultimately quite devoid of substance and who was subsequently roasted by Sabine Prokhoris[3] in her book *Au bon plaisir des «docteurs graves»*.[4] Her colleague Andrea Dworkin is, in fact, also part of the pantheon of feminist icons, proving herself capable of writing that '*Under patriarchy, every woman's son is her potential betrayer and also the inevitable rapist or exploiter of another woman*' (*Our Blood*) and that '*[[S]ex] is often a hostile act, often an exercise of power over somebody else.*' (*Norah Vincent, Sex, Love and Politics*).

This type of discourse is particularly pronounced among third-wave and, starting in 2010, fourth-wave feminists, who encourage women to free themselves from male influence and to question the traditional family model and even heterosexuality itself. Marriage and motherhood are sometimes perceived as forms of slavery. Heterosexual intercourse, even of the consensual kind, is considered rape because it perpetuates male domination. Thus, the exploration of alternative sexualities is advocated so as to achieve 'empower-ment', which consists in one's individual acquirement of social power by freeing oneself from norms and idealised femininity, a projection that is purported to be typically masculine.

In short, from the perspective of any contemporary feminist, the enemy is necessarily male. Modern feminist rhetoric and the de-nunciation of oppressive patriarchy as being the primary explanation

---

3   TN: Sabine Prokhoris is a French psychoanalyst and philosopher.

4   TN: At the Pleasure of 'Serious Doctors'.

behind all personal and social difficulties are indeed a source of comfort, an intellectual and psychological convenience coupled with a prestigious cause for one to join. One feels both rebellious and provocative while remaining comfortable with one's weaknesses or failures. And that is what accounts for the popularity of such attitudes. Being a man is thus equivalent to being an oppressor and being granted privileges by an inherently patriarchal society. Being a woman, by contrast, is almost ontologically equivalent to being a victim, a victim subjected to this structural patriarchy that drags one down. The oppressor/victim binary scheme is therefore highly similar to the one that leads to the denunciation of white privilege. The only difference is the change of adversary. White norms on the one hand, male norms on the other.

The combination of such feminism with racial issues was first theorised in 1989 by Afro-feminist academic Kimberlé Williams Crenshaw. It was in her desire to denounce both white privilege and male privilege that she coined the concept of *intersectionality*. Her goal was to highlight the interactions between several types of discrimination, the foremost of which were those suffered by African-American women. Doubly victimised for being both women and black, they thus experienced greater difficulties than white women, who remained privileged.

At the time, feminism was dominated by white activists and intellectuals. In Crenshaw's eyes, this situation made the greater suffering of black women go unnoticed. Such is the criticism still levelled at white women today, however supportive of minorities they may be. Under no circumstances should white feminists believe themselves immune to this widespread, destructive enterprise — for in the eyes of their current allies, they are more white than they are women. Once the white man is defeated, they are the ones that shall constitute the next targets.

Why? Because intersectionality allows victimisation to accumulate and reinforce itself. According to American 'body-positive and non-binary' activist Sonalee Rashatwar, the only way to defeat *fatphobia* would be to 'dismantle Western civilization'. Oh, just that, huh? Everyone wants their moment of fame and the struggle is fierce. There are dominant individuals everywhere and it's a matter of who will end up suffering the most. One thus coins catch-all terms to denounce multiple oppressors: *misogynoir,*[5] *heteropatriarchy*, *whitetriarchy*... Is a black man discriminated against more or less than a white woman? And what about Arab Muslims, who are not renowned for embracing feminism — are they oppressors or oppressed? In this game, black, poor, Muslim, transgender, lesbian, disabled, autistic, and obese women do not have it easy by any means, but in terms of social prestige, they've surely hit the jackpot.

Intersectionality as a Political Strategy

Initially, the political left's rapid adoption of the intersectional prism had both tactical and ideological dimensions. Indeed, the left had abandoned the white proletariat, deemed guilty of refusing to carry out the promised revolution. It thus sought out a substitute, a replacement 'proletariat' capable of fulfilling the Marxist prophecy. Racial struggle thus overlapped with class struggle.

In the words of Éric Zemmour, the left's 'revolutionary ideology' has found its 'revolutionary people': immigrants, who are victims of white domination. In accordance with extreme-left discourse, both immigrants and their societies are more or less conflated with the old adversary, namely capitalism. Immigrants, however, are not yet numerous enough for the left to claim power through the ballot box.

Intersectional strategy, which was first adopted by the American left, was dubbed a 'coalition of the fringes' by paleo-conservative thinker Steve Sailer. The idea here is to designate the heterosexual white man as the shared enemy of several constituencies — including

---

5   TN: A combination of the French words *misogynie* (misogyny) and *noir* ('black').

non-whites, women, LGBT people, Muslims, etc. — in order to push them to perceive themselves as oppressed minorities that must unite to take revenge. Following America's lead, this approach quickly spread to countries that had been greatly affected by immigration, such as the United Kingdom, Germany, Sweden, Canada, and, starting in the early 2000s, France, of course, through Terra Nova, a socialist think tank.

As a tool for the social analysis of overlapping oppressions, academic intersectionality has thus been coupled with struggle-based intersectionality. Also referred to as a convergence of struggles, it has enabled the union of the concepts of woman-subjugating patriarchy, LGBT-oppressing heterosexual domination, and that of a white privilege that dominates racial or religious minorities. Although originally more a matter of 'political politicking'— as elected left-wing officials courted Muslim voters— French Islamo-leftism is now closer to such attitudes thanks to the intersection of various community demands that hold the left captive.

At times, the societies desired by far-left activists, de-colonial blacks, LGBT feminists, and Islamists categorically contradict each other in terms of their respective agendas. These groups, however, mostly manage to unite because their primary goal is to destroy the prevailing white, oppressive, bourgeois, patriarchal, and racist system, their shared adversaries being European man and his civilisation. On the occasion of a demonstration held on 1 May 2018, the Afro-feminist collective Mwasi thus called for the formation of a *non-mixed racialised procession [...] against savage, racist, ableist, misogynistic, and classist capitalism, as well as against state racism and hetero-whitetriarchy*!

Intersectionality would, however, quickly reveal its limits, as during that same year, the Mwasi collective declared in its Afro-fem manifesto that it rejected 'white feminism'. Divides are indeed emerging, as seen with the TERF (Trans-Exclusionary Radical Feminist) movement. In the eyes of these radical feminists, men in skirts are not women, but remain males trying to attract social and media attention. These trans people should thus not be associated with the feminist struggle, but rather excluded from it, because they overshadow real women. Similarly, the Islamists of the Collective against Islamophobia in France do not take kindly to 'female imams', just as Gay Pride parades in the suburbs are not to everyone's taste.

Originally largely white, feminist, pro-LGBT and believing it could rely on intersectionality to gain political ground (a strategy which, according to Steve Sailer, brought Barack Obama to power), the left now finds itself increasingly dominated, both intellectually and politically, by exogenous components it once believed it could seduce and manipulate: Black people in the United States, Islamists in Europe. Overwhelmed by the racial issue amidst an ideological headlong rush promoted by its fanatical young watchmen with religious overtones, the Western political left is becoming more radical in its criticism of white privilege.

III

WOKEISM, A RELIGIOUS PHENOMENON

GET WOKE!

Former US President Joe Biden is a good example of this dyed-in-the-wool left that thought it could fan the flames to its own benefit, only to end up badly burned. An old-school, centrist Democrat that had acted as a U.S. senator for 36 years before becoming the vice president of the United States of America for the entirety of the Obama presidency, Biden was known for his smooth, consensus-building personality. This was also partly why he would become, in 2020, the Democratic candidate against the particularly divisive Donald Trump. Indeed, Biden was supposed to embody balance, seriousness, and a return to normalcy.

His campaign, however, gradually take on a wokeist tinge. The term 'wokeism' is actually derived from 'woke', meaning 'aware' in African-American vernacular dialect. It is a corruption of the English word 'awake', which has the same meaning. Beginning in 2014, when the Black Lives Matter movement started gaining momentum, the word 'woke' became a concept symbolising the African-American community's awakening to certain social issues, a rallying cry against systemic racism and white privilege. Wokeism has ironically come to refer to a phenomenon affecting a whole segment of the population, whose members are often white, affluent, urban, educated, and left-oriented.

Generally described as bourgeois or progressive, and imbued with feminist doctrine, the latter is eager to prove its sensitivity to the suffering of racial minorities and its readiness to be their 'ally'. This emotional fragility is also characteristic of woke activists, particularly young people who are offended by everything and demand safe spaces or trigger warnings to protect themselves against anything that might potentially shock them.

The Black Lives Matter movement would grow further after several African Americans were shot dead by police officers, mostly under legitimate circumstances, garnering media attention. Amidst all the emotion, the media propaganda, and the protesters' activist frenzy, the 'woke' mentality would spread like a virus from the extreme left to more moderate Democratic voters.

It is, in fact, wokeism that introduces the idea that white privilege does indeed exist and that this privilege is invisible to those who benefit from it, which opens the door to all sorts of abuses. White leftists have thus gradually submitted to the increasingly extreme rhetoric of black activists and intersectional feminists, who explained to them that racism was ubiquitous and that the United States and the entire West were both founded on white supremacy, which had to be eradicated. Despite acting as allies, these bourgeois bohemians were thus themselves racist without realising it and had to deconstruct their privileges and their own civilisation.

This groundswell, which candidate Hillary Clinton attempted to take advantage of in 2016, would exert a profound influence on the American left. It was indeed this very electorate that Joe Biden was faced with in 2020: people convinced of the existence of white privilege and of a nation that was not only inherently racist, but also deeply patriarchal, homophobic, and Islamophobic as a result of the intersectionality of discrimination. Without any qualms, Biden, who had, until then, been an exceedingly moderate figure, began to express his support. He even admitted that he himself had benefited from white privilege and knelt before some Black Lives Matter protesters. He also proceeded to choose Kamala Harris, who hadn't even dared to participate in the Democratic Party's primaries because of her poor poll numbers, as his vice president.

The choice was simple, as Harris was a Black woman, yet not too much so, since she had, for a long time, been much more willing to highlight her Indian ancestry. It was, in fact, a community niche like any other, and Kamala Harris only began to genuinely exploit her African heritage a few years ago, out of sheer opportunism. It was the right move for her, as she is now hailed as having been the first woman, the first African-American, and the first Indian-American vice president of the United States. The fact that Kamala Harris is, above all, an emblematic representative of the American elite, just as Obama was, doesn't seem to make any difference. A black woman — talk about progress!

One thing led to another and Joe Biden soon became a prisoner of 'wokeness', giving in to the most extreme segment of his electorate. To please them, he even appointed transgender Rachel Levine, formerly known as Richard, to be his Assistant Secretary for Health. Following the legal verdict that convicted Derek Chauvin, the police officer accused of having caused the death of George Floyd, Biden went so far as to state that 'systemic racism' was a 'stain on our nation's soul'.

The Genealogy of a New Morality

Such vocabulary is quite reminiscent of the notion of original sin. Indeed, wokeism has all the attributes of a vibrant religion permeated by dogmas that sometimes stir up violent protests, rather like early Calvinism. A professor at the University of South Dakota, Joseph Bottum, who is also active as an author and a specialist in political religious phenomena, has devoted an entire book to the topic, titling it *An Anxious Age: The Post-Protestant Ethic and the Spirit of America* in (a reference to the famous book by sociologist Max Weber).

Bottum believes that the de-Christianisation — the 'disenchant-ment of the world' of which Max Weber spoke — of American society, which came about later than in Western Europe, has not neces-sarily weakened the Protestant mentality. Having become a kind of Puritanism without God, it has shifted towards boundless devotion to minorities, particularly black people, who, as former slaves, are ever the victims. Wokeism is thus a manifestation of this post-Protestant-ism. Bottum summarised part of his theory in an interview with *Le Figaro* in September 2020:

> We now have a Church of Christ without Christ. This means that there is no possible forgiveness. In the Christian religion, original sin refers to the idea that one is born guilty, that humanity inherits a burden that corrupts one's desires and actions. Christ, however, pays our debts of original sin, freeing us from it. If one removes Christ from the picture, on the other hand, one gets... white guilt and systemic racism.

White privilege is thus the new original sin, for which one can no longer even be redeemed or forgiven. According to Canadian jour-nalist Barbara Kay, whiteness studies profess that one can '*mitigate one's individual white privilege, but not eradicate it. The goal is to ingrain a sense of eternal non-white victimisation and eternal white guilt*'. Just as feminism proclaims 'Yes, *all* men', implying that all men participate in the dominant patriarchy, wokeism states 'Yes, all whites'. All whites are alleged to benefit from and perpetuate the white supremacy that characterises European civilisation. All of us are racists, all of us sinners.

A new Great Awakening — a term describing the various waves of religious revivals that have swept through Anglo-Saxon societies since the early 18th century — now exported to all white countries, wokeism has its own dogmas. The first of these is obviously the existence of white privilege rooted in racism. There are, however, other aspects to it that also fall under the wishful thinking category, such as the belief that non-whites cannot actually be racists. Within the woke conception of things, racism is not, as previously stated by Peggy McIntosh, so much an individual act of meanness or discrimination as it is a system. To be guilty of racism, one must both cause harm and be in a socially dominant position. This is the now-enshrined pseudo-sociological equation according to which racism = prejudice + power.

Since ethnic minorities in the West lack political, cultural, and economic power, they are not racist in the same sense that White people are, even though non-White individuals may indeed discriminate against others or commit acts of hatred. Moreover, white people simply cannot be victims of racism. As sociologist Éric Fassin explains, 'When you label someone a filthy white person, what does that actually resonate with? Not much at all. It does not refer to any racist history. For there is no racism without domination, and as a group, white people have never been dominated in France.'

Rapper Nick Conrad, who chants 'Hang the whites' and 'I kill white babies', is, therefore, not racist. The young woman gang-raped in Évry in March 2014, targeted by her attackers 'because she was French', and the young and mentally disabled white man tortured for hours in Chicago in 2017 by four black men who filmed themselves shouting 'Fuck white people', will both be relieved to find out that their ordeal was not in any way motivated by racism. There's white privilege for you. Thank you, Éric Fassin!

In the same vein, observable facts become negligible: for woke people, it is an indisputable reality that the police are racist. This is true even if statistics prove that, each and every year, fewer black people are killed by the police than white ones — in 2020, 23% of those killed by the police were Black, 45% were white — and even if studies show that American police officers are more hesitant to shoot black suspects for fear of being accused of racism.

The woke religion also has its own priests, namely propagandist journalists and activist academics working in a vaccum in the field of social sciences. Resenting any questioning of their work, they eagerly and uncritically quote one another, publishing ever more extremist theories. In 2018, three intellectuals seeking to denounce this system put together a hoax by submitting several papers to various academic journals, particularly targeting the field of gender studies. Intentionally grotesque topics and content, including 'Rape Culture among Dogs in Dog Parks' and a rendition of an entire chapter of Hitler's *Mein Kampf* rewritten in feminist jargon, were thus published!

Additionally, the Great 'Awokening' has its own rituals as well: one must publicly kneel, ideally before black representatives of the new chosen people, to perform penance, reflect on things and prove that one is not racist. Many white leftists are now submitting to this, none more so than Joe Biden, as mentioned above. American and British police officers have also knelt before black protesters in order to appease them.

Even Champions League football players, Euro 2021 national team players, and rugby players at the Six Nations Tournament knelt in such a manner. Some still refuse to do so, but how long before they are forced to by their clubs or under activist pressure?

Even more noticeable is the sanctification of African Americans killed by the American police. They are, however, almost always repeat offenders, yet are somehow canonised upon their death and celebrated through street riots or media eulogies, all repeating the same mantra alleging that the man in question '*was a good boy who didn't deserve to die*'. The same thing can be observed in France whenever an Afro-Maghrebian offender dies while trying to flee the police. The Adama Committee's poster girl, Assa Traoré,[1] is granted every conceivable virtue and has even been celebrated in *Time Magazine*. The most remarkable figure, however, remains that of George Floyd. The place where he died, now symbolically re-baptised 'George Floyd Square', acts as the primary holy place of the Woke religion. Several

---

1   TN: Adama Traoré's half-sister.

signs set the rules that one is to follow, as people are urged to enter in silence and show respect for the place, with white people in particular expected to mind their behaviour. Some pastors even perform on-site baptisms, as 'miracles' are said to occur there. Saint George Floyd and Saint Adama Traoré, pray for us!

Last but not least, wokeism has its own eschatology: our earthly paradise is within reach. All one needs to do is to simply abolish white privilege. Since this privilege is the keystone of racism, patriarchy, capitalism, Islamophobia (in a word, of the entire demonised West), it is the root of all socio-racial tensions. If hundreds of black people attack, destroy, and loot everything as part of some Black Lives Matter protests, if some of them brutalise or kill white people for no apparent reason, it's because they feel oppressed and are fighting back as best they can. If Afro-Maghrebian thugs set French neighbourhoods ablaze, it's because they are disadvantaged. We must show them understanding. If Islamists long to throw homosexuals off the roof of a building, or if black people start attacking Asians deemed too successful in the United States, it's because the capitalist Whitetriarchy antagonises these groups in its desire to perpetuate itself!

Once the white system has been destroyed, racial or cultural inequalities and tensions are bound to naturally subside. White man represents the obstacle that stands in the way of the world's return to the Garden of Eden, preceding the invention of racism, sexism, and capitalism. Everything will turn out well once whiteness has been deconstructed and eradicated: such is the millenarian promise of wokeness, its promised bright future. Historian Noel Ignatiev, a pioneer of whiteness studies, already mentioned as one of Theodore W. Allen's acolytes, was a graduate of Harvard University, where he would later go on to lecture. His position was no different:

> The key to solving the social problems of our age is to abolish the white race, which means no more and no less than abolishing the privileges of [the] white skin.

Once the white race has been abolished, peace and abundance shall reign.

In his blog, soberly titled *Race Traitor: Treason to Whiteness is Loyalty to Humanity*, Ignatiev absolves himself of any hatred by assuring people of the following:

> We do not hate you or anyone else for the colour of your skin […] When we say we want to abolish the white race, we do not mean we want to exterminate people with fair skin. We mean that we want to do away with the social meaning of skin colour, thereby abolishing the white race as a social category.

The white race is thus only singled out as a social category, a designation necessary for sociological study. Incidentally, like gender, race is presented by the same radical left as a purely socio-cultural construct with no biological basis. It does not necessarily overlap with skin colour.

The choice of words is not insignificant, however. Why designate the white race and white skin as objects of vindictiveness in the first place? And even if these were truly just intellectual conceptions on the part of well-intentioned sociologists committed to simple social justice, how can we believe that this type of discourse, one that requires contrived subtlety, won't devolve into simple racial hatred?

This kind of rhetoric, which remains typical of detractors of white privilege, skilfully maintains the confusion between the insidious discriminations of white privilege, the socio-cultural norm of whiteness, the West as a civilisation, and last but not least, the white race or its members. Such vagueness allows us to swear that we have nothing against individuals of European descent while openly stirring up hatred towards them, since they are continually designated as being simultaneously the creators, representatives, and vectors of this abhorred white privilege. In a 2002 article for *Harvard Magazine*, Ignatiev himself wrote that '*[t]he goal of abolishing the white race is on its face so desirable that some may find it hard to believe that it could incur any opposition other than from committed white supremacists'.*

No method, however, is considered too extreme in the face of white supremacy, i.e. in the face of structural racism regarded as much as a global system of discrimination and oppression as an existential threat to the physical safety of non-whites. Karl Popper's paradox of tolerance, a benchmark of the violent far left, comes to mind: *'If we want a tolerant society, we must be intolerant of intolerance'.* Such rhetoric sets the stage for racially motivated attacks such as those already seen in South Africa against the Boers. For the time being, this aversion takes on the form of cancel culture in the rest of the West.

Cancel Culture: White Scare

Just like any religion, wokeism has its fanatics, those heralds of 'diversity ideology' analysed by sociologist Mathieu Bock-Côté and whose purpose is to hunt down heresy and strive to destroy it. Has someone said one word too many? Has someone's gesture been misinterpreted? Is there a possible racist ulterior motive? Well, that's where thousands of social justice warriors will attempt to identify the culprit, reveal their identity on social media, harass them, call their job to have them fired, or even protest in front of their home. As Joseph Bottum says, *'Previously, we were excluded from the Church; today, we are excluded from public life.'* This is what is known as cancel culture, a genuine neo-McCarthyism in which the 'red scare' has turned into a 'white scare'. Beware the white person that offends minorities!

In 2012, the Colorado-based Masterpiece Cakeshop was one of the first high-profile victims of such media and social media hate campaigns for refusing to bake a cake for a same-sex wedding. Other examples include Kiersten Hening, who was kicked off her college football team for refusing to kneel in tribute to the Black Lives Matter movement during a pre-game ceremony. Or US Army Sergeant

Jonathan Pentland, who was harassed after being filmed asking a young African-American man displaying suspicious behaviour — a man who, we later learnt, was known to the police for suspected sexual assault and attempted child kidnapping[2]—to leave his neighbourhood and pushing him, somewhat manfully but without causing harm. The next day, more than a hundred people crowded under Pentland's windows to vandalise his home, insult him, threaten him, and demand accountability. Abandoned by his superiors, he was also charged with assault.

In the Netherlands, controversy prevented a white translator from translating a book by Amanda Gorman, a black author, following an article by black activist and journalist Janice Deul, who found the choice of a non-black translator 'incomprehensible'. In *The Simpsons*, white actor Hank Azaria, the long-time voice actor for an Indian character, had to stop and apologise:

> I apologise for my part in creating that and participating in that. Part of me feels like I need to go to every single Indian person in this country and personally apologize. And sometimes I do.

Cancel culture also takes on the form of mass censorship on social media, sometimes outright social blacklisting for violating political correctness. In France, Génération Identitaire and hundreds of anonymous accounts have suffered such a fate. In the United States, things have gone as far as censoring US President Donald Trump, banning him from all digital platforms and even some banks. Several of his supporters involved in the 6 January 2021 protest and the symbolic storming of the Capitol have been banned from using various airlines.

In March 2017, Bret Weinstein, a biology professor at Evergreen College in Washington State, was the victim of a vicious intimidation

---

2   TN: At the time of the incident, the man, who was later identified as Deandre Williams, had obviously not been indicted yet. This seems to have changed in the meantime.

campaign with the aim of forcing him to resign. He had openly criticised a proposed modification to the traditional 'Day of Absence', during which non-whites deliberately abstained from attending school in order to implicitly demonstrate their contribution. Indeed, an administrator had suggested that white people stay off campus for a day,[3] which Weinstein called a dangerous 'logic of oppression'. Woke activists immediately gathered and, following a blockade that almost got out of hand, seized power in the faculty and forced the leadership team and professors to hold a public repentance session in which they had to acknowledge their privileges. Police subsequently advised Weinstein against returning to campus, in their belief that he would be in danger there.

The story is reminiscent of that of two professors at IEP[4] Grenoble, harassed and labelled 'fascists' in March 2021 by some Islamo-leftist members of the UNEF[5] for having challenged the idea that Islamophobia was similar to racism and anti-Semitism. Also in France, cartoonist Xavier Gorce fell victim to cancel culture as a result of one of his drawings which mocked the debates surrounding the incest case involving political scientist Olivier Duhamel. Afro-feminist Rokhaya Diallo criticised the drawing for the crime of transphobia. As for *Le Monde*, it quickly removed it from its online publication, without informing Gorce, and apologised. The phenomenon is now accelerating, and the cases are already beyond count.

The woke inquisition doesn't just stigmatise non-believers, sometimes destroying their social lives. Becoming increasingly zealous and intolerant, it is trapped in a mechanism called a 'purity spiral', analysed by sociologists Bradley Campbell and Jason Manning in their book entitled *The Rise of Victimhood Culture*. Even neutrality is considered complicity. Cultural and intellectual terrorism, which is

---

3   TN: Allegedly to focus on issues of race.

4   TN: Institut d'Études Politiques (Institute of Political Studies).

5   TN: Union Nationale des Étudiants de France (National Student Union of France).

now becoming more and more fanatical, does not tolerate the slightest dissent. It displays totalitarian and violent tendencies reminiscent of Leninist Bolshevism.

Attacking both its opponents and its lukewarm supporters, wokeism purges its own ranks by excommunicating both schismatics and doubters. Old-style left-wing activists or intellectuals who refuse to fall in line with de-colonialists (such as *Printemps républicain*[6]) and who do not even half-heartedly acknowledge the existence of white privilege quickly find themselves classified as part of the far right. In France, one case is emblematic in this regard: that of *Charlie Hebdo*.[7] A long-standing icon of the Left, the magazine and some of its columnists are now accused of fascism and Islamophobia. This last accusation has also been aimed at Samuel Paty.[8] And we know what the outcome was.

Another notorious victim of cancel culture is J. K. Rowling, author of the bestselling Harry Potter series. Owing to a tweet deemed transphobic, she found herself ostracised by the woke community in 2020. Previously viewed as a icon of the progressives, she had long been considered flawless, going as far as to attribute homosexual tendencies to one of her main characters ex post. Similarly, during a 2016 play set in the Harry Potter universe and casting a white character in the role of a black actress, Rowling claimed — wrongly, some readers would point out — that she had never explicitly defined her character as white.

---

6   TN: *Printemps républicain* (Republican Spring) is a French political movement founded in 2016 with the intention of fighting against 'the far right and political Islamism' and defending secularism.

7   TN: The satirical magazine that published caricatures of the prophet Muhammad and whose cartoonists (5 in total) were subsequently slaughtered by Muslim gunmen.

8   TN: Samuel Paty was a secondary school teacher who allegedly showed his students some of the Charlie Hebdo caricatures of Muhammad during a lesson on the topic of freedom of speech. In response, he was killed with a cleaver by an 18-year-old Muslim 'refugee'.

However, by subsequently expressing the view that 'biological sex is a reality' and that 'people who menstruate' can simply be called women, she transgressed one of the tenets of wokeism: the belief in the absolute disconnection between sex and gender. An intense controversy ensued: in the press, in feminist circles, within her fan community, and even at her French publisher's, Hachette, some of whose employees refused to work on her next book. To cap it all, the black actress she had supported a few years earlier also supported Rowling... before withdrawing under the pressure!

In order to smear someone, woke inquisitors go as far as to search for tweets dating back several years. This, however, only goes one way: in 2018, *The New York Times* was singled out for hiring journalist Sarah Jeong. Indeed, internet users had found anti-White tweets dating back to 2014, such as: '*Oh man it's kind of sick how much joy I get out of being cruel to old white men*'. Some even contained the hashtag '#CancelWhitePeople'. *The New York Times* defended its choice and chose to keep Jeong. Had the tweets been anti-black or Islamophobic, there's no doubt that Jeong would have been fired on that very same day.

Going even further, wokeists actually attack personalities or works that are decades or centuries old, denouncing their racism or sexism, sometimes even demanding their redaction or revision. *Sleeping Beauty* and *Snow White*? Both are sexist, since in both cases the prince 'rapes' the woman by kissing her without her consent. And what about the children's books penned by Dr. Seuss, who died in 1991? They were deemed racist and withdrawn from sale. Shakespeare? 'Hateful', according to American author Padma Venkatraman, who is significantly less talented than the great English playwright. Jean-Baptiste Colbert and his Code Noir,[9] which was an

---

9   TN: France's *code noir,* or black code, was a set of legal articles originally drafted during the 17th century by French First Minister of State Jean-Baptiste Colbert and later completed by his son, Jean-Baptiste Antoine Colbert.

objective step forward for slaves? Racist — his statues should be torn down, just like those of American Confederate generals.

In its philosophy, this phenomenon is reminiscent of the iconoclasm of the early Christians and 14th-century Protestants who destroyed idols, or, more recently, the frenzy of the Islamic State, whose members demolished museums, as well as the site of Palmyra, because they served to remind the world that something did actually exist before Islam. In its practice, it is also similar to the Roman *damnatio memoriae*, on the basis of which politicians were condemned to oblivion and erased from both records and art for crimes against the state. The eternal damnation of wokeism falls upon all those who are suspected of the crime of racism, whether today or at any point in history. An unqualified sort of literalism, one that refuses to recontextualise statements in their own period, is at work here.

What greater symbol of cancel culture than the proposal put forward by the prestigious English University of Oxford to remove Homer and Virgil from its classical studies curriculum? A choice already made by a certain Massachusetts university, where a certain professor stated that she was '*very proud to say that [they had] removed* The Odyssey *from the curriculum*' that year.

Commissioned by King Louis XIV, it aimed to manage the lives of both slaves and masters in French Caribbean colonies.

IV

AN IDEOLOGY OF RESENTMENT

Wakanda Forever: Afro-Centrism

IN APRIL 2018, French Afro-feminist activists Rokhaya Diallo, Amandine Gay, and Danièle Obono—a member of the *La France Insoumise* party—had their photo taken in the courtyard of the National Assembly. They had gathered there for the screening of the documentary film entitled *Ouvrir la voix*, directed by Amandine Gay herself, which gives voice to several black women recounting their various experiences. In a 2016 interview with *Le Monde*, Amandine Gay explained:

> We are always on alert, because if we ever forget that we are black, we are reminded of it in an extremely violent way. For those who grow up in an environment where being white is the norm, it is extremely difficult to understand what black people experience in France.

The daughter of a Martinican father and a Moroccan mother, Amandine Gay, later adopted by white people living in the Lyon countryside, moved to Montreal, Canada, because she found 'nothing in France that could make black children proud'. The screening of her film at the National Assembly, thanks to the involvement of MP Obono and Diallo's support, was therefore a personal victory. This fact is reflected in the pose adopted by all three of them in the photo, where they can be seen with their arms crossed over their chests and their closed fists touching their shoulders.

This stance is taken from *Black Panther*, a Hollywood film released a few months earlier. A big-budget production centred on the eponymous Marvel Comics superhero, *Black Panther* was a genuine social phenomenon in the African-American community. And for good reason: all the protagonists are black, as the story takes place in Wakanda, an imaginary, contemporary African country located between Ethiopia, South Sudan, Uganda, and Kenya.

In the story, Wakanda is preparing to crown its prince and grant him the title of Black Panther, a title borne by its founding king, a warrior who had gained superpowers through contact with a meteorite metal thousands of years earlier. Uniting several African tribes, the first king was, thanks to the mentioned metal, able to ensure the progress of his nation, allowing it to become very advanced technologically while disguising itself as a third-world nation. Having reclaimed the usurped throne as Black Panther at the end of the film, the new king appears at the UN and reveals the true nature of his country, which then takes its rightful place in the community of nations.

A stable, wealthy, and powerful kingdom that is technologically advanced and hidden away so as not to arouse the envy or jealousy of other nations, Wakanda embodies all African aspirations. It is a fantasy that reflects what Africa could have allegedly been in the absence of white colonisers. What is remarkable is that three of France's most prominent Afro-feminist activists have chosen to espouse Wakanda's rallying sign in front of the National Assembly. The symbolism is clear: black people are awakening; they are proud, free, and Wakanda is in the making. Were it not for white privilege, they would have built it ages ago!

White privilege is often used as an excuse for the failures of many non-whites, particularly Africans. Instead of finding pride in their unique ways of life and social expressions, which are different from those of other civilisations but equally honourable, many Africans cling to the idea that their continent would be more prosperous had it not experienced white colonisation. This tendency sometimes leads to the advocacy of untenable theories belonging to the Afro-centric current.

Largely based on the work of Senegalese historian Cheikh Anta Diop, Afro-centrism is an academic movement generally criticised for its militant nature. In contrast with Africanism, which is primarily a Western and biased perspective on Africa, Afro-centrism aims to enable the scientific, historical, political, and cultural emancipation of both Africa and the African diaspora.

The best-known Afro-centric theory was formulated by Cheikh Anta Diop, who published his first work in 1954 under the title *Nations nègres et culture: de l'Antiquité nègre égyptienne aux problèmes culturels de l'Afrique noire d'aujourd'hui* [1] This theory, marginalised by almost all historians and geneticists, claims that ancient Egypt was actually a 'black civilisation', thus calling into question the ethnicity of the Egyptian population at the time by asserting that it was allegedly composed of a majority of black people. Diop also defends the notion of a cultural unity in sub-Saharan Africa that pre-dated colonisation and that can be rediscovered. This imaginary unity is now part of the mental matrix of most African Americans, just like the supposed black origin of Greek philosophy or the establishment of significant contacts between pre-Columbian America and Africa, which is alleged to have greatly influenced the former.

At the same time, Afro-centrism asserts that the contribution of Africans to humanity is grossly underestimated, sometimes even deliberately. White historiography thus tends to denigrate or conceal the rich history of Africa, as well as the scientific contributions of black people. Long lists of inventions or major scientific innovations

---

1   TN: *Negro Nations and Culture: From Egyptian Black Antiquity to the Cultural Problems of Black Africa Today.*

attributed to black people regularly appear on the internet — almost
all of which relate to African Americans who, therefore, were educated in white countries.

To name just a few, Lewis Howard Latimer is said to have revo-
lutionised the electric light bulb, giving rise to the one we know today; Alexander Miles is claimed to have given birth to the modern
elevator; Thomas Elkins is alleged to have invented refrigeration and
freezing systems; Andrew Jackson Beard is said to have invented, in
1892, the combustion engine — which had actually been produced as
early as 1854! The list is long, mentioning, one by one, inventions that
have affected all of humanity. The only problem is that when you look
more closely, all the people thus highlighted had actually filed, at best,
a simple patent to slightly improve on an older invention conceived
by a white person.

What is even more incongruous is that, according to some Afro-
centrists, black people have always been numerous in Europe,
although the political authorities have always tried to conceal this.
Beethoven, in particular, was supposedly black, a belief that remains
widespread today among the African diaspora in the West. The claim
is based on a handful of rare accounts that are purported to date back
to the period and that were published in 1944 by Jamaican-American
journalist Joel Augustus Rogers, one of the founders of African-
American studies. In a most vague fashion, these accounts describe
Beethoven as having a 'dark' complexion.

This was enough to for them to let their imagination run riot
and present him as being African, despite all the paintings that de-
pict the great composer. Several prominent figures of the American
movement to abolish segregation in the United States echoed this
sentiment, including African-American nationalistic activist and
spokesperson for the Nation of Islam, Malcolm X, who already spoke
of the 'white devil' and would claim that Beethoven's father 'was one
of the Blackamoors that hired themselves out in Europe as professional soldiers'. As for the American music magazine Rolling Stone,

it went so far as to publish a 1969 article titled 'Beethoven Was Black and Proud'!

These are but a few examples, among many others, of the extremes to which Afro-centrism, which suffuses a part of the pseudo-academic field of black studies, actually leads. Devoid of any and all rational critical thinking and fuelling a vast conspiracy theory alleging that white people have been obscuring history and taking credit for other peoples' achievements (a ploy that supposedly entrenches white privilege), Afro-centrism is wreaking havoc in the black community.

A Victim Mentality

There is, however, a blatant paradox at the heart of such theories. If Africa was so advanced and so powerful, if it did indeed produce so many geniuses, how is it that it ended up becoming what it is today? The answer is 'obvious': being too generous, open, and incapable of racism, Africa allowed itself to be deceived by white colonisers, who have since been trying to erase its history and have profoundly altered its ethno-social balance. Hence, in part, the difficulties it now faces in terms of recovery.

The fundamental issue with Afro-centrism is that it combines the legitimate desire to approach African history from an African perspective with the claim of revealing a past that is alleged to be as prestigious as that of other continents. Rather than accepting and valuing Africans for what they were and actually are, this resentful approach concerns a desire to rewrite history, fuelling all sorts of fantasies.

Africans, whether living in Africa or the West, need to adopt a clear-eyed perspective of themselves and be guided by the dismal failure of Liberia, a country founded by freed African-American slaves who voluntarily re-migrated to Africa. In sharp contrast to such an attitude, hatred of the West largely stems from a victim mentality, a position in which activists for the Black cause actually wallow. The persecution syndrome that can be discerned behind the denunciation

of white privilege and that is used as an excuse or a way to minimise
the failures of Africans applies both to the past and its Afro-centrism
and to the contemporary era with the myths of neo-colonialism.

Africa is thus said to still be under the authority of whites, who
have never truly decolonised the continent. This idea is based primarily on the artificial delineation of the borders of sub-Saharan
Africa, a legacy of the Europeans who deliberately created hetero-
geneous, multi-ethnic, and multi-religious states with the aim of
limiting their capacity for emancipation. And yet, while it is indeed
true that African borders were determined by European colonisation,
there are two things that one must bear in mind.

The first is that most of the African continent has, historically speaking, rarely experienced statal organisation. Naturally, states
have, of course, existed, including the great empires of Ethiopia — a
very particular empire alleged to have been founded at the end of the
10th century and to have persisted, in various forms, until 1974 — and
Mali (from around 1235 to 1600), or even the Zulu kingdom of the
19th century. Overall, however, these entities were, on the one hand,
concentrated in the fertile region of western Sudan, extending from
modern Senegal to Nigeria, with the rest of the sub-Saharan continent remaining largely tribal. On the other, these states were, most
of the time, rooted in the domination of a majority or more powerful
ethnic group over the others, a principle that is encountered in modern African states and their democratic game, which often amounts
to a mere balance of demographic power.

Moreover, they were often connected to the trans-Saharan cara-
van trade of the Muslim world, thus fuelling the slave trade for over a
millennium, and then to the Atlantic slave trade, and finally, towards
the mid-19th century, to the oil trade. Ultimately, borders remained
blurred, with territories taking on the shape of controlled zones with
variable, rather than genuinely demarcated, frontiers. African borders
are indeed artificial and recent, since they did not, mostly, even exist
beforehand.

Secondly, African elites were not mistaken in the fact that the formation of states in the aftermath of decolonisation afforded an opportunity to establish modern administrations and societies. Indeed, it was the Africans themselves who decided to maintain such a division. When the Organisation of African Unity was established in 1963, two coalitions began to clash: the Casablanca Group, led by Ghanaian President Kwame Nkrumah, who favoured a redesigning of borders and pan-African federalism, and the Monrovia Group, united behind Senegalese President Léopold Sédar Senghor.

Senghor expressed a preference to maintain the prevailing territorial status quo in order to safeguard the newly independent African states, hoping to transform them subsequently into nation-states. It was his vision that would ultimately triumph and, during a meeting in Cairo, African heads of state decided to 'respect the sovereignty and territorial integrity of each state and its inalienable right to an independent existence'. The following year, on 21 July 1964, they specified, in a joint resolution, that 'all Member States pledge themselves to respect the borders existing on their achievement of national independence'.

African borders were therefore freely accepted by Africans themselves. To complain about them today as a white conspiracy whose aim is to keep the continent in a state of subjugation is nothing short of a fallacy.

Indeed, the borders could certainly be redrawn in a manner that is more in line with the reality of African ethnic groups, but it is African leaders who do not wish this to happen. Complaining about borders is purely a matter of contemporary political debate, just like the independence aspirations espoused by some Scots or Flemish people. The fact of using this argument to explain Africa's failures also allows one to readily forget that the continent was not exactly opulent or powerful prior to colonisation. Whether it can be so today depends primarily on the Africans themselves.

There is, however, another imaginary persecution of which the West is accused, namely the plundering of Africa and the maintaining of the white yoke through economic means. And it is France that is most often singled out and accused of perpetuating a type of 'France-Africa', particularly through the CFA franc[2]—the disappearance of which is, incidentally, already scheduled. It is, in fact, an actual boon for the countries that use the currency, as their stability is guaranteed by France (as is its parity with the euro), thus preventing sudden devaluations and limiting inflation. Far from being prisoners, several African countries have already relinquished the CFA franc without any incidents and without having their economies experience significant improvement. Twenty-two years after replacing the CFA franc, Mali even reversed its decision and reinstated its use in 1984.

Nevertheless, the CFA franc is often presented as a way for France to keep user countries within its fold. And yet, in 2019, as pointed out by Africanist Bernard Lugan, *'the CFA zone as a whole, including Sahel countries, represented barely more than 1% of all French foreign trade'*. This is a far cry from the plundering that is regularly claimed. Such plundering is also alleged to take on the form of resource control, particularly in the case of Niger-produced uranium. While France does indeed obtain a large amount of its uranium from Niger, representing 40% of its uranium imports in 2017, it is more of a provided service than anything else, simply because this uranium, like all other raw materials, is traded: it is simply bought!

And it is not bought cheaply, either: Kazakhstan, by far the world's largest producer with more than a third of all mined uranium worldwide, sells it almost 30% cheaper than Niger. Such trade is, therefore, mutually beneficial, since France obtains its supplies from a reliable partner whose sites it actually protects — by shedding the blood of its soldiers in the fight against Islamic terrorism in the Sahel,

2   TN: 'CFA franc' is the name given to two distinct currencies used by 210 million people across fourteen African countries.

for instance, all at the request of African leaders — before actually buying its resources at exorbitant prices. This situation is also reminiscent of Algeria's, a country from which France continues to buy low quality oil (totalling 12% of its imports) to prevent the country's economic collapse.

If there is indeed any plundering, it is rather that of the West at the hands of Africa: according to the World Bank, $82 billion was transferred in 2017 from developed countries to Africa and the Middle East through the latter's diasporas. These transfers represent, for example, approximately 12% of Senegal's GDP and a net loss for the countries of origin. Moreover, the OECD estimates that developed countries send approximately 55 billion in development aid to Africa every single year, including 2.9 billion in the case of France and approximately 10 billion in the case of the United States in 2020. Given the corruption that plagues the black continent, this money is often embezzled.

To speak of the plundering or domination of Africa at the hands of the West, when goods are being purchased at global rates and white countries send billions of euros in aid each year without any compensation, is simply absurd. Such victimhood-based discourse — which, incidentally, minimises China's growing predation in this part of the globe — serves, above all, to portray white people as perpetual villains, thereby serving as an excuse for the difficulties which Africa and the African diaspora face when it comes to taking charge of their own lives.

Deconstructing Everything — Destroying It All

Just as white privilege is perceived by progressives and intersectional activists as the main obstacle preventing the resolution of all social inequalities and the supposed discriminations that result from it in European countries, the West is also seen as hindering Africa and the black diaspora, paralysing their racial and civilisational empowerment. The alleged historical, political, cultural, and economic oppression implemented by white people is said to be, on the one hand, responsible for preventing the black people that live in white countries from becoming their equals in all respects, and, on the other, for delaying Africa's development.

Instead of fostering the advancement of their own communities and empowering them, black activists complain of being kept at the bottom of the social hierarchy. In doing so, these activists lock themselves in and wallow in the position of inferiority that they actually denounce: rather than seeking to develop solutions and improve their situation, they prefer to attack whites, who they expect to renounce their own identities, as if this could consequently emancipate black people.

Adding to these demands, especially in Western Europe, are the promoters of political Islamism. Often funded by Muslim-Arab countries and organised in particular by the Muslim Brotherhood networks and the Turkish Millî Görüş movement, they fuel this type of discourse with a view to achieving civilisational revenge and applying a well-thought-out strategy of conquest, as explained by the essayist Alexandre del Valle in his book entitled *Le Projet*.[3] Their activists, indigenists and de-colonialists ever on the hunt for 'Islamophobia', which they equate with racism, are often members of the Maghreb diaspora and very well connected with the traditional political and academic left. Born as an offshoot of the Muslim Brotherhood and now dissolved, the Collective against Islamophobia in France (CCIF) was particularly representative of this movement.

Ever the focal point of this resentment campaign, white people find themselves increasingly denigrated. Everything Western is alleged to be rooted in racism. And it is for this reason that everything Western must be targeted with condemnation: lifestyle, science, arts, history, you name it—for all of these elements come together to constitute whiteness. Indeed, there is nothing that could escape the

---

3   TN: The Project.

condemnation aimed at white privilege, which must be challenged and deconstructed everywhere: the West must be de-Westernised and de-whitened.

Classical music is too white: such is the opinion of some professors at the British University of Oxford, who are calling for a reform that would allow them to distance themselves from the classical repertoire (including Mozart, Schubert, and even poor old Beethoven, who has certainly experienced some rather odd things) on the grounds that it focuses on 'white European music dating back to the age of slavery'. The teaching of music theory 'has not been freed from its connection to its colonial past', causing 'great distress to students of colour', who take it all as 'a slap in the face'. Classical music, therefore, needs to be 'decolonised'. The American media have been making similar observations: *The New York Times* has accused classical music of masking a 'racist issue', while the National Public Radio recently wondered why it was 'so white'.

Mathematics is also deemed too white. In the US state of Virginia, the Department of Education announced in April 2021 that it was removing all advanced math lessons for classes that precede the 11th grade — the equivalent of the *'première'* in France — owing to the fact that they lack diversity. In February of that same year, Oregon had promoted a training toolkit for teachers that bestows upon the teaching of mathematics 'toxic characteristics of white supremacist culture'.

The course, titled *Pathway to Math Equity: Dismantling Racism in Mathematics*, targets 'ethno-mathematics' and argues that 'white supremacy manifests itself in the focus on finding the right answer' [while] '[t]he concept of mathematics being purely objective is unequivocally false'. Indeed, due to its 'colonisation', 'math is used to uphold capitalist, imperialist, and racist views'. This 'equitable math' program has received a $1 million grant from the Bill & Melinda Gates Foundation!

On the occasion of the bicentennial of his death, Napoleon was vilified both in France and across the Atlantic as a paragon of white supremacy — a supremacy that is alleged to have shaped all of Western history. In an op-ed published in *The New York Times*, Marlene Daut, an American academic of Haitian descent, called upon France not to celebrate Napoleon, 'the architect of modern genocide' and 'an icon of white supremacy'. In *The Washington Post*, Rokhaya Diallo considered 'Macron's decision to commemorate Napoleon [as] an insult to France and its people', on the grounds that he was 'racist and misogynistic'. An immigrant from Cape Verde, Élisabeth Moreno, Emmanuel Macron's Minister Delegate for Gender Equality and Diversity, was unsure whether to celebrate the bicentennial of 'one of the most misogynistic writers [she had] ever read'. Far from limiting themselves to the Emperor, these activists view all of Western history through a contemporary woke lens.

The study of European antiquity, an academic field that the Anglo-Saxons term 'Classics', is thus widely criticised. Dan-el Padilla Peralta, a renowned professor of Roman history, is a black man from the Dominican Republic who teaches at Princeton University. At a 2019 conference, he stated that '[t]he production of whiteness turns on closer examination to reside in the very marrows of Classics'. He hopes 'the field dies, and that it dies as swiftly as possible'. The university agreed with him, deciding that Greek and Latin would no longer be compulsory in Classics.

Peralta is joined by Johanna Hanink, associate professor of Classics at Brown University, who sees the study of antiquity as a 'both a product of and [a] long-time accomplice in violent societal structures, including white supremacy, colonialism, classism, and misogyny', and by Donna Zuckerberg, a Ph.D. in Classics who finds herself wondering whether we can save a 'discipline that has historically been implicated in fascism and colonialism' and that 'continues to be enmeshed in white supremacy and misogyny'. In the eyes of Nadhira Hill, a doctoral candidate in art history and archaeology at the University of Michigan, 'classics is toxic'.

These are but a few prominent figures. Indeed, in the eyes of an entire rising generation of scholars, all of Western history is to be re-examined through modern morality. They shamelessly commit what has long been considered the most egregious historical error imaginable: the anachronism of judging the past by the standards of the time.

For its part, the Canadian government has since 2021 required its diplomats to undergo training which explained that 'objectivity', 'perfectionism', 'the worship of the written word', and 'meritocracy' are harmful. These founding traits of Western civilisation, which one might generally consider desirable, are an integral part of the 'culture of white supremacy'. Distributed by the *Toronto Sun*, the official anti-racism training material of the Department of Foreign Affairs repeats the doctrine of critical race theory word for word. It states that 'if you are not an anti-racist, you are complicit' and that non-whites may indeed have 'racial prejudices' such as 'white people [being unable] to dance', but this does not constitute racism because of the 'systemic relationship to power' It also adds that '[i]n Canada, white people hold this cultural power due to Eurocentric modes of thinking, rooted in colonialism, that continue to reproduce and privilege whiteness'. These 'training' efforts are managed by a government 'equity' programme worth more than 300 million Canadian dollars.

Urged to embrace change by several hundred of its employees, the *Opéra de Paris* — 'considered a fortress of tradition', according to de-colonial activist Françoise Vergès — is opening up to diversity; its general director, Alexander Neef, agreed that 'one cannot refuse to evolve' and asked experts to reflect on the notion of 'white ballet, the archetype of classical ballet'. *Marie Claire* magazine echoes this sentiment, asserting that 'ballet is unbearably white', because, to quote former black dancer Theresa Ruth Howard, it propagates the idea that 'desirability, fragility, and sexual purity' are the 'ideal of white womanhood [...], the epitome of beauty, of grace, and of elegance, and these are not adjectives that are assigned to black women'.

In the same vein, the Sierra Club, an American environmental NGO that is said to have 3.8 million members and supporters and organizes expeditions to discover the country's natural heritage, has spoken of the 'unbearable whiteness of hiking'. In an op-ed published by *The Guardian*, one of Britain's leading daily newspapers, playwright Lucy Prebble complained that '*video games [had to] 'change'*, because '*[r]ight now they are too white and too male*'. In one of its articles, *Marie Claire* magazine deemed space and NASA 'too white'. Writing in *The New York Times*, historian Natalia Mehlman Petrzela expressed her belief that '*jogging has always excluded black people*'.

The list is already a long one, and one can readily wager that it won't stop there. All the cases mentioned are far from isolated anecdotes stemming from marginalised groups. Indeed, they show that nothing can escape the war being waged against white privilege. If there is systemic racism, however, it is the one that actually targets white people. In the name of the struggle against racism, cancel culture attacks everything related to white cultures. As Henri Levavasseur says, it is '*a movement that should rather be called* culture cancel: *it is not a "culture of erasure", but rather an "erasure of culture"*' — that of whites, obviously. The claim of deconstructing everything does a very poor job at concealing the desire to destroy everything.

V

THE VIRTUE SIGNALLING OF THE WESTERN BOURGEOISIE

The Elite's Ideology

ON THE American CBS network, Emmanuel Macron stated in April 2021 that the French had to 'deconstruct [their] own history'. According to him, France suffers from racism as a result of its colonial past, *'the issue of race [lying] at the very heart of our societies'*. He had already asserted that 'French culture does not exist' and that 'being a white man can be experienced as a privilege'. Echoing the vulgate of critical race theory, Emmanuel Macron is emblematic of this white upper bourgeoisie imbued with contempt for its own people and history.

Whether by conviction or calculation, the Western elite quickly adopted this anti-white doctrine. Americanised and bottle-fed on liberal progressivism, it was already fully committed to diversity ideology: the idolisation of minorities, multiculturalism (which Canada has even incorporated at the constitutional level), LGBT fetishism, a fascination for Islam, openness to all ideas and cultures, etc. The idealised figure of the 'Other', of the one who is not a white man and has come to regenerate the old world deemed guilty of the worst crimes, unites with that of the interchangeable individual within a

fluid society of abstract economic vision. It is a global village, a global
market whose members are all avid iPhone consumers.

The mental representations of the Western elite are American
ones. This ideological homogenisation was achieved through standardised education, through television and film culture, through the
examplification of economic success, and through language, i.e. the
international *Globish* necessary to bring about commercial globalism.
Since the end of the Second World War, the United States has been
perceived as a land of liberators, protectors, and leaders of the 'free
world'. Obama is 'so cool', Silicon Valley so high-tech, Jeff Bezos so
successful, and all that our gilded youth can think about is getting an
MBA at universities across the Atlantic... How could Western leaders
fail to see American society as a model? Indeed, their dream is for
Europe to become the 51st American state. And thanks to them, it is
already America's mental colony and protectorate.

Both critical race theory and its denunciation of white privilege
have been superimposed on this very matrix. The election of Donald
Trump on the basis of his anti-immigration rhetoric was akin to
electroshock therapy for the white hyperclass. Didn't Trump's victory prove that the United States was still racist? The fact that Obama
had preceded him doesn't change a thing, as racism remains clearly
prevalent among whites. We must therefore redouble our efforts to
eradicate it.

In the eyes of the Western bourgeoisie, Trump's accession to the
White House validates the discourse against white privilege more
than the death of any George Floyd. Black Lives Matter, for instance,
was only one embodiment of the prevalence of such ideas. Indeed,
the movement had emerged following the theoretical elaboration of
structural racism within the leftist intelligentsia and the conversion of
elites who all attend the same universities, embrace the same lifestyles
and espouse the same cultural and intellectual references. The arguments and demands voiced by those that protested against alleged
police violence were not organic, but rather derived from a political

and semantic corpus already honed by academics, the media, and political activists.

Idealising diversity is convenient when one is not exposed to it. It is all the easier for the bourgeoisie to denounce white privilege and support the demands of ethnic minorities when its members are not in contact with the latter. The most dominant individuals are part of this pseudo-elite class that imposes its self-righteous discourse and political correctness out of naiveté, conformity, or conviction. This is rather normal when it comes to those who, generally speaking, do not suffer the anguish of a multiracial and multicultural society: out of sight, out of mind. It is the most privileged ones who, thanks to their moral authority, constantly criticise the supposed privileges of unfortunate whites.

The world of culture, primarily the sphere of American cinema and music, is the epitome of this bourgeoisie, a bourgeoisie that had long been sheltered from the diversity ideology that it so outrageously promotes. Angelina Jolie is a caricature of this: a bisexual woman involved in humanitarian work and sporting tattoos in English, Latin, Arabic, Chinese, and Khmer, she is the mother of six children, three of whom are adopted and of Cambodian, Ethiopian, and Vietnamese descent. One of her own daughters was even presented as transgender, asking to be called John from the age of two!

The 2021 Oscars ceremony was a High Mass of the dominant ideology, with actors taking to the stage to mourn the death of George Floyd, applauding the verdict that had convicted the police officer accused of having caused his death and expressing outrage at systemic racism. As for viewers, they did not tolerate this: viewership thus plummeted by 60% compared to the previous year, highlighting the growing divide between the woke hyperclass and those that it regularly targets with its self-righteous sermons.

Already enjoying an almost hegemonic status among the Western elite, this discourse is now infiltrating every aspect of our lives. In 2021, on the occasion of the International Day for the Elimination of Discrimination, the world's No. 1 and No. 4 chess players played a gala match at the initiative of UNESCO, allowing the black side to start. The NBA created the 'Kareem Abdul-Jabbar Award' to reward basketball players that act as 'social justice champions'. In 2021, the French dictionary publisher Éditions Larousse included, for their part, the term 'racialised' in their list of new words. A term dear to both Rokhaya Diallo and Françoise Vergès, 'racialised' is defined as follows: 'Someone who is the object of racist perceptions or behaviours'. Marginal politicised concepts have thus become generalised observations.

The most decisive role in this paradigm shift is certainly played by the media, with rare exceptions that are ideologically — and racially — homogeneous. So much so that left-wing sociologist Éric Fassin pointed this out in an interview with *TV5 Monde*: '*Take the media world, for example. Officially, almost everyone is anti-racist, but in practice, almost everyone is white.*' According to him, this is blatant evidence of systemic racism. Delphine Ernotte, the CEO of France Télévisions, had already stated in 2015 that France had '*a television network of white men over 50, which needs to change*'.

Left-wing media outlets are the vanguard of wokeism. They preach the good word, spewing forth entire waves of mental cramming whose intensity is matched only by the contempt they hold for the white working classes, which they perceive as racist and fascist. Acting as the system's 'new watchdogs', to use the words of Serge Halimi,[1] journalists are largely cut from the same bourgeois and left-wing sociological cloth. During the 2012 French presidential election, a Harris Interactive survey showed that in the second round, 74% of all surveyed journalists had voted for François Hollande.[2] At France's two largest journalism schools, namely the Lille School of Journalism

---

1   TN: Born in 1955, Serge Halimi is a French author and journalist.

2   TN: François Hollande is a socialist French politician who served as President of France between 2012 and 2017.

and the Paris Journalism Training Centre, students voted for the Left in 87% and 100% of all cases respectively!

The astonishing 2017 media propaganda in favour of Emmanuel Macron found its match in the 2016 American presidential campaign. In total, 500 newspapers and magazines expressed official support for Hillary Clinton, with only 28 backing Trump. Even fewer supported Trump in 2020 against Joe Biden, with barely 23 endorsing the incumbent president. Even the prestigious scientific journal *Nature* took a stand by supporting the Democratic candidate for the first time in its history.

As for wokeness itself, what better example could one find than *The New York Times*, one of the world's leading newspapers? Until 2014, it had only mentioned 'whiteness' in about 0.25% of its articles, according to the analysis company LexisNexis. In 2018, the term surfaced in nearly 2% of them. In July 2020, the magazine's editorial team even decided to capitalise Black but not white in its articles '*because white doesn't represent a shared culture and history in the way Black does, and also has long been capitalised by hate groups*'. This decision was then echoed by many other press publications.

Last but not least, television is undoubtedly the most powerful vector of the dominant ideology. In France, its high priest is Yann Barthès, who sets the tone with his consummately Parisian shows filled with soothing political correctness. In the United States, this role is assumed by famous show hosts Oprah Winfrey and Rachel Maddow, the MSNBC star, as well as by the late-night talk shows of Stephen Colbert, Bill Maher, and Jimmy Fallon. These shows, combining politically engaged commentaries with uncontroversial humour, mould the political consciousness of urban bobos, pushing them down the slippery slope of wokeness.

The Comfort of Conformism

Nowadays, although it is fashionable to be feministic, anti-racist, pro-LGBT, eco-friendly, vegan, and Islamophilic while mocking white males, it is even trendier to show it, i.e. to proclaim it loud and clear. This behaviour is typically a form of ostentatious virtue, which Molière portrayed in his *Tartuffe*, otherwise known as *The Impostor*. The Anglo-Saxons have recently revived the idea by speaking of 'virtue signalling' to describe the propensity of progressives to openly express their opinions or sentiments. This phenomenon, which affects both the elite and the average urban bourgeoisie, has been significantly exacerbated by social media, through which bobos can signal their virtue to the rest of the world, regardless of whether it's sincere or hypocritical!

The Chinese have a word for progressive whites who seek to flaunt their moral virtue. They call them the *baizuo*, which means 'white leftist' or 'white progressive'. They are arrogant and condescending, regarding themselves as morally superior and, as such, in a position to lecture the entire world: the *baizuo* is the archetypal metrosexual bobo on an electric scooter, who proclaims himself left-wing without being particularly militant. If de-colonialists and woke activists are now spearheading the war against white privilege, the *baizuo*, whether Hollywood jet setters or junior service sector executives full of xeno-oestrogens, are the bulk of the troops that follow without questioning.

Georges Bernanos[3] had already denounced them in *La liberté, pour quoi faire?*[4]: '*Their submission to progress is matched only by their submission to the State [...], and progress exempts them from ever straying from the path followed by everyone else.*' The Chinese media portray the *baizuo* as people who only care about issues such as minorities, LGBT rights, and the environment, with no grasp of the real problems affecting the majority of their own people. They promote peace and equality to satisfy their sense of moral superiority, while

---

3   TN: A Catholic with monarchist inclinations, Louis Émile Clément Georges Bernanos was a French writer and a soldier in World War I.

4   TN: Freedom — For What Purpose?

reamining so obsessed with political correctness that they tolerate the backward values of Islam in order to preserve multiculturalism.

When mentioning this last trait, it's hard not to recall the scandal surrounding Muslim grooming gangs, most of which are of Pakistani origin and have been operating in the United Kingdom since the early 1980s. Despite the numerous testimonies and evidence, neither the police and social services, nor the political authorities have shown any willingness to act, for fear of coming across as racist. A journalist investigating these rapes was forced to undergo a workshop on racism and diversity. Tens of thousands of young white women have suffered the worst possible abuses in Rochdale, Telford, and Rotherham, all in the name of multiculturalism and political correctness, and the show biz sphere has failed to mobilise and defend them. How many networks of this kind still exist?

Virtue signalling is not just a way for people to boast. Often involving unconscious mechanisms, it is also a strategy that allows one to acquire social capital by making themselves look good and showing off that they champion just causes. Moreover, being 'on the right side of history' allows one to join the side of the winners, that of the dominant ones. Denigrating white privilege is fully in line with such social and psychological comfort.

It's a simple and risk-free way to acquire social prestige. A white leftist that denounces white supremacy and structural racism — how brave! It is nothing more than elitist moralisation worthy of poodles. One fights against oppressive windmills to give themselves the impression of standing out from the crowd, just like a billionaire that promotes ecology and cycling while actually owning a private jet. As Philippe Muray[5] once said, the right-thinking ones never slip, because they are actually the ice.

In addition, conformity is also a sexual strategy: indeed, woke issues resonate particularly well with left-leaning women. Since they

5   TN: Born In Angers (France) in 1945, Philippe Muray was a French essayist and novelist.

tend to be more sexually open and to marry or have children later in life, they represent a larger pool of potential sexual partners. And since you have to sell yourself to bourgeois women steeped in anti-racist feminism, you proceed to signal your virtue... That's progressive courtship for you. Peacocks show off, deer bray, frogs croak, and metropolitan soybean men make it known that they find the gender pay gap scandalous or that they cried upon learning of the death of George Floyd.

Political correctness is a powerful mechanism. If you repeat something over and over again, you end up adhering to it. Often acting on pure conformism so as not to stand out, professions of faith are eventually internalised and become genuine beliefs. During the Korean War, many American prisoners in the hands of the Chinese communists underwent such a psychological process: instead of torturing them, their captors demanded small political concessions. In exchange for small rewards — food, cigarettes, walks — they made them say or write that 'the United States was not perfect'. They also asked them to list some of the problems plaguing capitalist societies. The prisoners thus made small, harmless, and sometimes even sincere compromises with the enemy. In doing so, they entered into a mental pattern of collaboration, harmless at first but destined to grow further.

A New Moral Order

Once you've put your finger in the cogs, you're often permanently trapped. And to resolve the discomfort of cognitive dissonance, that of things one does not believe in, the human brain ends up wanting to believe. When one experiences themselves saying or doing something, their mental image of themselves is changed and they end up wanting to conform to how they now perceive themselves. It's mentally more comfortable and easier to live with.

This new moral order also benefits from a psycho-physiological mechanism openly exploited by social media: popular posts generate notifications, which in turn trigger endorphin rushes, creating a feeling of pleasure. As with a drug, the user is driven to always want more. There are, in fact, two effective ways to receive such physiological gratification on social media. The first, which particularly affects teenage girls and delights predators, is to adopt hyper-sexualised behaviour in order to gain virtual attention. More accessible to left-leaning white adults, the second consists in conforming to the dominant ideology. This interaction between virtue signalling and its reward (on the one hand, in the shape of social prestige, and on the other, through hormonal and moral remuneration) fosters woke indoctrination.

As a dominant ideology, political correctness also has another weapon: shaming. Psychologists use the term 'socialisation' to refer to the process through which children are encouraged to think and act the way society demands. This education is carried out through a shaming game whenever they make comments or behave in ways that go against our society's moral code. This moral code weighs so heavily on people today, especially when one is a left-leaning white person, a *baizuo* ashamed of their own race and ancestors, that it becomes difficult to avoid a constant feeling of guilt.

American anti-racist activists have even coined the expression 'white guilt' to encourage white people to blame themselves for the 'sins' of their ancestors. Those who criticise white privilege readily rely on this aspect of guilt to impose their discourse and demands more effectively. Foreign agents such as *Al Jazeera* (Qatar) and *Anadolu* (Turkey) even exploit this guilt as a soft power tool. In this regard, Mathieu Bock-Côté[6] speaks of neo-Maoism, referring to the *'self-flagellation sessions of artists and other socialites who accuse themselves of being improper allies in an increasingly ostentatious expiatory ritual'*.

---

6   TN: Now residing in Paris, Mathieu Bock-Côté is a Canadian sociologist, essayist, author, public intellectual, and conservative political commentator.

White progressives are now beating their breast and indulging in self-criticism so as to stay on the side of the good guys, the 'allies' of minorities, rather than give the impression of being part of the racist camp. This subservience will, however, do them no good, as submission never pays and they will be asked for more and more contrition. In *Un coupable presque parfait. La construction du bouc-émissaire blanc*,[7] Pascal Bruckner[8] reminds us that *'nothing arouses more rage than a man who has fallen to the ground. Already hated for its past domination, the West is now despised for its decline'*.

Acceptance of the various aspects of progressivism and the above-mentioned white guilt, including the dogmas of critical race theory, is, in fact, a process of power and structural domination, which is exactly what white privilege is criticised for. Should one publicly reject even one of the precepts of wokeness, the result may very well be ostracisation and marginalisation from one's 'good' society, as already seen with cancel culture.

Beyond the abuses of woke revolutionary guardians, however, the dominant ideology perniciously imposes itself on everyone: while social media act as an amplifier for social gratification in the name of virtue signalling, it also encourages self-censorship, since discussing sensitive topics carries the risk of public humiliation. Progressives can live their lives with unconcealed faces, whereas their opponents risk being pilloried if they reveal themselves. Digital anonymity is thus the last bastion that protects what little remains of freedom of expression in the West.

Those who do not particularly seek to defend ideas also suffer from this social pressure and moral domination. Even if they are not fully aware of it, they have no choice but to adhere to the dominant discourse or, at least, say nothing against it, thus allowing it to spread without any opposition. In 1987, the deconstructionist Gilles Deleuze

---

7   TN: The Almost Perfect Culprit: The Moulding of the White Scapegoat.

8   TN: One of the "New Philosophers" that acquired prominent status in the 1970s, Pascal Bruckner is a French author.

anticipated the advent of what he called 'societies of control': '*We are not even being asked to believe, but rather to behave as if we did.*' Is allowing people to say that a cross-dressing man should be able to play rugby on a women's team (genital ablation is no longer even necessary in this respect) or that non-whites are victims of systemic racism such a high price to pay when what is at stake is a person's ability to keep the job that allows them to feed a family? Conversely, default acceptance, ever palpable in the apathy of the masses that mechanically embrace fashionable ideas and influencer trends, is often rewarding and costs nothing.

In no way is this soft liberal-progressive totalitarianism a deliberate social engineering project. The conditioning of minds that it induces is simply the result of social and psychological mechanisms that exert intense socialisation pressure on individuals. So much so that on 6 January 2021, American teenagers denounced their own parents for marching outside the Capitol in support of Donald Trump, resembling George Orwell's *1984* or the heyday of Russian communism.

Initially a mere amalgamation of liberalism and anti-racism, the ideology of diversity was long limited to the dogmas of the individual — '*There is no such thing as society*', said Thatcher — and multiculturalism. Possessing real institutional power, it is now spurred on by critical race theory, which permeates the political class, the media, culture, and academia. The dominant ideology imposes its precepts; the fact that it does so while denouncing an alleged white supremacy that is clearly struggling to resist it is nothing but cruel irony.

V I

THE ANTI-WHITE
WORKING CAPITAL

A Marketing Strategy

THE VICTIM narrative built on white privilege and critical race theory is also being spread through marketing. In parallel to their conquest of the Western elite, various anti-racist, diversity-related and ultimately woke doctrines were perfectly absorbed by financial capitalism. Wokeism quickly became a commercial strategy, allowing consumers to be targeted. It thus manifests itself in two main manners.

The first is that of *blackwashing*. The term itself refers to a practice that has become commonplace both in films and on television, where white historical or fictional characters are played by black actors. Conversely, having white actors play black people is no longer tolerated: *blackwashing* is inclusive, while *whitewashing* is racist. In marketing terms, *blackwashing* consists in giving the brand in question a pro-black and, more broadly, a pro-diversity image. It is similar to *greenwashing* and *pinkwashing*, wherein brands emphasise their focus on environmentalism and LGBT issues in order to project a positive image, even if the product has nothing to do with such topics. Through *blackwashing*, non-white people and their values are highlighted to attract racialised and anti-racist customers.

It is also a means for activist groups to exert pressure, with these groups filing racism-related lawsuits against brands that do not sufficiently advocate diversity and are thus not to their liking. One thinks back to 2019, when *Le Slip français* was attacked on social media because the company only had white employees. The brand quickly complied, apologising for the fact that 'there wasn't much diversity in the team' and stating that they 'would like that to change'. Disgraced, Le Slip has since turned this attitude into a real marketing choice, no longer releasing any ad without at least one African person, while proclaiming its commitment to diversity whenever the opportunity arises. Even without ideological or commercial ulterior motives, it has become imperative to nuance one's communication in order to avoid being suspected of white privilege and fend off the stigma that goes hand in hand with it.

The second marketing angle, one that is still relatively uncommon but has been gaining momentum, is *whitebashing* (the denigration or pillorying of white people). The company that most shamelessly exploits this strategy is the American ice cream brand Ben & Jerry's, a subsidiary of the food giant Unilever. Having started with now-classic themes (including support for socialist candidate Bernie Sanders in 2016, the promotion of same-sex marriage on its packaging, support for illegal immigrants, etc.), the brand shamelessly appropriated the vocabulary of critical race theory in the wake of George Floyd's death. Thus, taking sides in connection with the pro-Trump demonstration held on 6 January 2021, Ben & Jerry's tweeted: 'Yesterday was not a protest — it was a riot to uphold white supremacy'. In April of that same year, after a police woman mistook her service weapon for a taser,[1] the company declared: 'The murder of #DaunteWright murder is rooted in white supremacy. [...] This system can't be reformed. It

---

1   TN: The police officer in question was Kimberly Potter, who stated that she had intended to use her service taser, but had instead shot Daunte Wright, a 20-year-old black American, during a traffic stop and attempted arrest for an outstanding warrant.

must be dismantled and a real system of public safety rebuilt from the ground up." All this to sell ice cream!

In June 2020, American pharmaceutical giant Johnson & Johnson, the owner of such brands as Neutrogena, RoC, and Le Petit Marseillais, terminated the sale of certain products that 'presented whiteness and light skin as more beautiful than other colours'. In the wake of this, L'Oréal decided to remove words such as 'white', 'whitening', and 'skin-lightening' from its products and communication, so as not to stigmatise its customers of colour. By betting on the precepts of anti-White rhetoric, these groups actually created a small media buzz amidst the Black Lives Matter protests, as part of a publicity stunt aimed at people of colour.

To varying degrees, many major brands exploit this dual niche of *blackwashing* and *whitebashing*. According to sociological and psychological studies on the topic, Europeans are the people with the least racial pride and are also the most self-deprecating. This is particularly pronounced among left-wing white people. They are therefore much less concerned about advertising campaigns that are detrimental to them or are adapted to target other races. Europeans do not resort to boycotts to economically sanction the multinationals that overplay the diversity card. And progressives go as far as to take advantage of this to signal their virtue by purchasing those multinationals' products. At the same time, other races are more driven to consume and more sensitive to advertising messages that emphasise them.

Based on all of this, the commercial logic of capitalism has, at the very least, a vested interest in not specifically targeting white consumers. In fact, however, while white people should generally be a core commercial target, since they still represent a vast majority in Western countries, advertising does not reflect this fact at all. We thus witness the almost systematic presence of racial minorities, particularly the ubiquitous white woman with black man combination. The opposite is scarcer, because it would symbolise white male domination over racialised women... An African man and a European woman, preferably blond: such is the caricature-like advertising couple that symbolises the modern, open and mixed-race society. As for Arab or Asian men and brown European women, they are rarely seen, because the visual gap would not be marked enough or sufficiently inclusive.

The same logic of harmonisation prevails in graphic design: many companies, especially in the start-up and tech spheres, have more or less the same visual digital communication. The result are scenes that are indistinguishable from one another, replicas that do not require any creative talent and are based on flat vectored shapes, representing asexual, coarse-looking, or disproportionate human bodies that are depicted in bright colours that often evoke neither race nor culture. At most, we can occasionally see an afro haircut or a wheelchair designed to fight against racism and ableism. Sometimes displaying simple smiles without any eyes or ears and thus unable to see or hear anything, these interchangeable individuals are happy. In the absence of identity, they are all identical. Such is the established graphic style of global homogenisation, i.e. *globohomo* art.

On social media, the logos of major corporations are all tinted black to surreptitiously appeal to Black Lives Matter and African consumers. They blithely wear the rainbow flag during Pride Month to support LGBT people — well, at least the subsidiaries located in the West do... What we have here is a standardisation of customers, products, and communication. Monthly deals allow all iPhone users to receive an oestrogen-laced Starbucks drink to go with their vegan burger, with 50 cents donated to BLM or the pro-transgender organisation of their choice! Talk about virtue signalling in the service of woke capitalism. *Globohomo Inc.* thanks you for your purchase.

All identitarian demands, except those of Europeans who only ask to be allowed to exist and remain themselves in the land of their ancestors, are thus incorporated into modern communication. Even the CIA and the US military forces have now joined in. In two decidedly woke advertisement videos, one can respectively see a 'cisgendered,[2] intersectional and anxiety-ridden' female CIA employee 'of colour' and a young female soldier 'raised by two mothers' participating in a Gay Pride parade. How distasteful: the female soldier is actually white... This could have been done better.

This struggle-related commodification generates some rather bizarre alliances. In a desire to castigate white workers and small business owners (who are necessarily racist), anti-capitalist, anti-fascist and Afro-feminist activists find themselves on the same side as Apple, Coca-Cola, Hollywood, and Wall Street. This comradeship doesn't seem to bother anyone. The 'Occupy Wall Street' protests against the '1%' are now water under the bridge — the fight against racism takes precedence over everything else. The political left has obliterated the issue of socio-economic inequality in favour of the fight against discrimination. The French embodiment of this woke capitalism is Louboutin,[3] showcasing Assa Traoré with her fist raised, thus implicitly signalling the definitive failure of the anti-capitalist left, which had hoped to manipulate racial minorities. Only massive boycotts led by whites could ever reverse this trend.

Often involving more ideas than interests, diversity-focused wokeness, however, is more than just a marketing ploy. This ideology is increasingly gaining power in various companies. This occurs when they recruit human resources officers or communication specialists formatted by the dominant discourse, or, as in some multinationals, when they go as far as to hire political commissars with degrees in gender or race theory to 'make a good impression'. Perceived as harmless and with a mission to ensure an inclusive professional environment where diversity and equality reign, they thus impose their whims: gender-neutral bathrooms, racial quotas among executives,

---

2   TN: Meaning not transgender.

3   TN: Louboutin is a luxury French fashion brand owned by designer Christian Louboutin and famous for its iconic stiletto heels with signature shiny, red-lacquered soles.

donations to left-wing associations, and even gender parity on their boards of directors.

This is also one of the reasons accounting for the prevalence of the advertising precepts described above. Since communicators are almost all formatted according to the same ideas and remain sociologically similar (urban, left-oriented metrosexuals and homosexuals who attended standardised communications schools), they generally propose and impose the same advertising scheme: two men of different races kissing. Even when it comes to selling burgers? Indeed, it really doesn't matter, as the product takes a back seat to the ideological message. What does matter is that one be modern.

And woe unto the bosses that try to refuse; these old and privileged white males are immediately denounced as being racist, sexist, or homophobic. Often, they simply allow things to unfold, because it's better than starting a conflict. After all, the damage is already done. And who cares, as long as business is good, right? Don't people repeat *ad nauseam* that diversity is a good thing for companies? A greater variety of personal experiences, diverse points of view, and original approaches are all assets to the company concerned! The only issue is that this seems to be part of the diversity mantra.

The reality is, however, quite different. In 2016, Alice Eagly, a professor of psychology and management at the renowned Northwestern University, published a study on the topic. Having examined several meta-analyses on diversity in business, she concluded that the correlation with improved performance was non-existent or extremely weak. Racial diversity even appears to be a real disadvantage at the level of society as a whole: in his now classic study *E Pluribus Unum: Diversity and Community in the Twenty-First Century*, Harvard professor Robert Putnam demonstrates that the more diverse a community is, the less its members trust each other. This is incidentally true both among different ethnic groups and within them. This reality is reflected in an entire host of factors: fewer close friends, less spontaneous cooperation among neighbours, less trust in law enforcement, reduced happiness and perceived quality of life, more time spent in front of television sets, etc. Although he had actually completed his work in 2001, Putnam admitted that he did not publish it until 2007 because he was trying to *develop proposals to compensate for the negative effects of diversity*'!

Despite all of this, the victim narrative that denounces white privilege is paying off. It works because it has managed to win over both the white bourgeoisie and multinational companies, while also paying literally, since the anti-white hype is also embodied in a more immediate form of business: the easy money that comes from whining.

Whining for Money

The struggle against white privilege is in itself a business. First of all, fighting against white men and their culture helps to maintain an academic ecosystem. The presence of entire legions of student-researchers in largely self-referential and redundant activist fields — black studies, whiteness studies, Chicano studies, gender studies, queer studies, trans studies, disability studies — produces thousands of mediocre sociological papers that no one actually reads. Relying solely on public funding for their survival, they serve as academic veneer for woke political demands.

Éric Fassin, whom we have already mentioned, exemplifies this caste of salaried far-left intellectuals who are paid to spit on white men. A graduate in English who has never defended a doctoral thesis but is nonetheless a lecturer at the Institute of Gender Studies at the University of Geneva, Fassin is a Judith Butler[4] specialist and an avowed intersectional activist with Islamo-leftist tendencies. He notably advocates the idea that discrimination does not even have to be demonstrated, since all oppression is necessarily real if it is felt by the oppressed. In his defence, this idea is widespread among

---

4   TN: Judith Pamela Butler is an American feminist philosopher and gender studies scholar.

wokeists: indeed, critical race theory embodies the reign of subjectivity. Anyone can be a victim and no proof is required as long as one feels offended. As previously stated, however, this does not apply to the victims of anti-white racism. Éric Fassin should have remained a rather unknown and verbose professor of postmodern philosophy, but the outbreak of racial tensions in the West has allowed him to present himself as an expert on white privilege, which he denounces on both *Médiapart*[5] and *France Culture*.[6]

Ridden with the disease of critical race theory, the left-wing activist community also thrives on donations and sometimes even generous public subsidies. Rarely showcasing any profiles that might otherwise legitimately claim high positions, it supports a whole host of professional whiners paid to advance their political ideas. Some even manage to build a real reputation and enjoy the profitability that goes hand in hand with it.

Having started from nothing, African-American Marxist activist Patrisse Cullors was kicked out of her parents' home at the age of 16 for revealing her queer preferences, before obtaining a degree in philosophy at the age of 29. Not exactly a brilliant path. Everything, however, changed when she co-founded the Black Lives Matter movement in 2013. She quickly gained fame and found herself propelled into the position of spokesperson for the black community: press reports, television coverage, awards, paid conferences, books, documentaries, partnerships, you name it — a commitment that proved lucrative, since between 2015 and 2020, she purchased no fewer than four large houses, including a $1.4 million villa located in an upscale white neighbourhood. Embarrassing revelations for an Afro-Marxist who immediately denounces racist attacks! Similarly, we are all bound to learn of the turnover of the Traoré family's victim business in a few years' time.

---

5   TN: Médiapart is an independent, non-profit French investigative online newspaper established in 2008.

6   TN: A public radio channel.

In France, it is Rokhaya Diallo that seems to be doing best so far. She was educated in an American school as part of an official US government programme to study diversity and learn its activist methods. Constantly denouncing the systemic racism of both France and the West, this self-declared 'intersectional and de-colonial feminist' did nonetheless obtain funding from the European Union and worked for our National Assembly's *LCP* channel. Invited everywhere, she has secured her place at *RTL*, *LCI*, *The Washington Post*, and *Al Jazeera*, a Qatari soft power instrument specialising in blaming whites. She is also a member of the board of directors at the Centre for Intersectional Justice, an NGO funded by George Soros's Open Society. Even the US Embassy in France promoted her audio show *Kiffe ta Race*[7] on Twitter, all despite her outspoken support for non-mixity, her criticism of 'white feminism' and her exclusion of white women from certain meetings, not to forget her ambiguity regarding radical Islam.

Evidently persecuted, Rohkaya Diallo was nominated in May 2021 by the Gender + Justice Initiative, a research group at the eminent Georgetown University in Washington, to be given a position 'as a researcher'. Although she will never strive for anything else but the destruction of European civilisation, she is now endorsed by an obscure academic group whose goal is to ensure that Georgetown truly addresses the 'issues of gender, race, and economic justice', not to mention 'sexuality, anti-racism, and social class'. It is all worthy of an anti-fascist tract.

Rokhaya Diallo, however, still remains in France to continue her work: having been granted the title of researcher, which is always prestigious when on a television set, she can continue her propaganda, adorned with an honorary title that grants her words a certain 'scientific' and 'legitimate' veneer. Less talented at selling themselves

---

7   TN: Dig your Race.

are figures such as Lilian Thuram[8] and Audrey Pulvar,[9] who commit one blunder after another while trying to wield the rhetoric of white privilege. Ever close to Anne Hidalgo, Pulvar, who was nominated for the 2021 regional elections by the Socialist Party in Île-de-France, believes that white people could perhaps attend non-mixity meetings as long as they keep quiet. How very kind. In the absence of the slightest subtlety, the mask is quickly removed to reveal plain and simple anti-white racism.

Another iconic figure is that of American 'diversity consultant' Robin DiAngelo, who has become a leading figure in the fight against white privilege thanks to her book titled *White Fragility: Why It's So Hard for White People to Talk about Racism*. The book reiterates an idea that she herself formulated in 2011, but the time was not right back then, it would seem. Published in 2018, the book went on to become a bestseller, bringing her both fame and millions of dollars.

Her discourse draws on her professional experience, which consists in giving seminars in companies to help employees 'work in a diverse environment.' In practice, this involves explaining to white people that they are racist every single day, '24 hours a day', and often unconsciously — such is the scourge of white privilege. DiAngelo's role is to help them become aware of this privilege. Her work was even used and offered to Coca-Cola employees as part of 'diversity trainings' in which they could learn how to be 'less white' and 'break with white solidarity'.

According to Robin DiAngelo, white people who feel neither racist nor privileged exhibit *white fragility*, a concept that neutralises any criticism. To be upset, angry, or simply sceptical when accused of racism is alleged to be tantamount to displaying white fragility and therefore one's white privilege. It's all a tautology, a circular argument

8   TN: A former professional footballer who now presents himself as an author and a philanthropist.

9   TN: Audrey Pulvar is a French journalist, television and radio host, and politician.

that can only be true when it adopts as its premise the very thing that it seeks to demonstrate: denying one's white privilege would thus amount to admitting it. The concept has, of course, flourished among woke activists.

DiAngelo goes even further when asserting in her latest book, entitled *Nice Racism: How Progressive White People Perpetuate Racial Harm*, that even those white people who actually acknowledge their privilege and champion anti-racism are not truly deconstructing their white privilege. They remain paternalistic, implicitly asserting their superiority by pretending to understand the suffering of black people when, in actual fact, their privilege prevents them from doing so. There's simply no escaping white privilege. Dismantling it takes 'a lifetime of conscious effort'. In DiAngelo's eyes, 'white people need to stop saying "I'm not racist"', because they are; every single one of them. All one has to do is keep quiet, bow down, and accept all criticisms expressed by non-whites as undeniable truths... and, of course, hand over one's money.

If resentment and the assumption of political power are the main motivations behind the anti-white movement, the lure of profit is not far behind. Indeed, when one looks past the individuals who profit from victimisation, the latter is a potentially lucrative tool for their entire communities. In fact, one of the major demands put forward by African Americans, one that also resonates with Africans living in Europe, is reparations.

There are actually three types of reparations. First, there is moral reparation, meaning repentance. Similar to the white guilt that must burden individuals, repentance extends to white colonising and slave-holding nations. Its goal is to subjugate these countries both diplomatically and politically, trapping them in a position of moral obligation and neutralising any and all criticism in advance.

Next in line is cultural reparation, involving the restitution of art objects and artefacts exhibited in European museums, items that are regarded as stolen. This is the path which Emmanuel Macron has chosen to follow, as some thirty objects were returned, the first of which was, symbolically, a sabre that had belonged to a black Muslim military leader who had fought against colonisation.

Last but not least, the most important type is obviously financial reparation. As descendants of martyred peoples, non-whites would be entitled to compensation in the form of hard cash. As for the amounts being proposed, they are exorbitant. For African-American economist William Darity, a 'reparations plan should eliminate the racial wealth gap, which was estimated to be an average difference of $840,900 in net worth between Black and white households'![10] Quite a steal, wouldn't you say?

Taking their Places

This idea of reparations poses another obvious problem: where does one stop? Can Italy demand reparations and the restitution of artefacts from Napoleon's France? Or should the descendants of the Gauls consider themselves victims of colonisation and genocide at the hands of Caesar's armies? As for the Iberian Peninsula and the Balkans, which were conquered and dominated by Muslims for centuries, who are they to submit the invoice to? All peoples have been colonisers and slave-holders, and all have colonised and enslaved others. And yet, only some black people and Islamists are still whining today.

Christiane Taubira[11] once attempted to include in her memory law on slavery the creation of a commission tasked with 'determining the harm suffered and examining the conditions for reparations due for this crime'. Displaying great skill in her preface to the book titled *The*

---

10   TN: As of 2019.

11   TN: Born in French Guiana, Christiane Taubira is a French politician who served as Minister of Justice in the governments of Prime Ministers Jean-Marc Ayrault and Manuel Valls.

Case for Reparations,[12] she clarified that 'no material reparation could ever erase a crime as great as slavery or colonisation'. White people must not be allowed to think that they could settle their imaginary debt and believe themselves to be even. Nothing will ever be enough. They will always have to consider themselves guilty and pay up, both materially and morally. The objective is clearly not to settle a dispute in order to start afresh on a firm footing, but rather to extract a victim's allowance from the past.

This attitude is, therefore, anything but naive and is actually a ploy. Far from being a virtuous struggle for emancipation and justice, victimhood leads to a kind of racketeering. As demonstrated by a major study published in 2020 by psychology researchers at the University of British Columbia, 'signalling victimhood is linked to a cluster of personality traits often considered immoral, including narcissism, Machiavellianism (a tendency to manipulate others), a sense of entitlement, and lower levels of honesty and humility'. According to them, the more a person presents themselves as a victim, regardless of whether this victimisation is justified, exaggerated, or simply false, the more inclined they are to lie, cheat, and denigrate others to gain certain advantages.

This sociopathic tendency is explored in the previously mentioned book entitled *The Rise of Victimhood Culture* by Campbell and Manning. They explain that 'victimhood is a social resource, a kind of status'. Victimhood is indeed an excellent social strategy, no matter whether it is horizontal, and thus a source of prestige and compassion, or vertical, i.e. promoting socio-professional advancement.

This efficacy is reinforced by the fact that humans have evolved anthropologically to display empathy in order to foster mutual aid and consequently community survival. Having lived for tens of thousands of years in a particularly harsh European environment due to its severe climate and hostile nature, white people have developed a

---

12 TN: The book is based on an article written by Ta-Nehisi Coates and published in *The Atlantic* in 2014.

particularly acute sense of empathy, an almost pathological type of altruism.

The exploitation of this altruism, with victimhood on the one hand and white guilt on the other, allows entitled racial minorities to take advantage of their hosts and reap benefits that traditional meritocracy would never offer them. This is essentially the very idea behind affirmative action. To compensate for discrimination, poverty or difficulties associated with certain social categories, the latter are structurally favoured through various measures: easier access to certain schools or professional recruitment, quotas or tax exemption policies, etc.

Implemented with a view to imposing equal opportunities, this inverted discrimination is harmful to the most deserving. In both academia and government, for instance, anonymous competitive examinations are the only guarantee of an objective assessment of people's performances. At school, however, selection is based on applications and thus allows for the selection of the most interesting candidates. By introducing affirmative action measures, the general educational level is decreased while simultaneously devaluing the diploma that validates the studies.

In the United States, students at major universities are recruited in accordance with a grading system that assesses the quality of the candidate: African Americans and Hispanics, regarded as being targets of discrimination and underrepresented, receive bonus points that allow them to take the place of more capable white or Asian students. Following in the footsteps of the Political Sciences Faculty under Richard Descoings, the prestigious French HEC[13] recently announced the introduction of such a 'bonus' system in the entrance exams of scholarship students that are deemed disadvantaged. Seeking to reform the ENA (National School of Administration), Emmanuel Macron is now also striving to reserve a quota of places for students

---

13   TN: *Haute École de Commerce* [literally 'Business High School'] the most prestigious business and management school in France.

that come from more modest backgrounds — i.e. those of 'immigrant origin' — in major administration schools.

Similar issues are encountered in the business field. Coupled with the fear of being accused of racism, the principle of affirmative action and recruitment-related 'diversity charters' favour the hiring of non-whites, who sometimes display less suitable profiles for the vacant position. Similarly, the diversity frenzy affects advertising and appointees, advantaging ethnic minorities and women in the name of diversity and making it more difficult for white men to advance professionally. For example, the American airline United Airlines has stated that it wants 'at least half of the new pilots trained at its United Aviate Academy to be women or people of colour', thus introducing a quota that is completely unfair to white, male pilots who are at least as deserving as that.

In the eyes of African-American economist Thomas Sowell, affirmative action has a blatantly negative effect. By facilitating the progression of ethnic minorities, it pushes them to rely on those quotas while robbing them of the means to make it on their own, thus creating a vicious circle. And yet, neither this phenomenon nor the obvious inequity of reverse discrimination that harms a certain part of the population seems to hinder our policymakers. Having barely been elected, US President Joe Biden implemented a relief plan for businesses struggling as a result of anti-Covid-19 measures, but he decided that white men would be the last to benefit from this aid, with priority given to 'Black, Latino, Asian, and Native American owned small businesses, [as well as] women owned businesses'.

In the cultural sphere, the 2022 Golden Globes ceremony would not be broadcast on its historic network, namely NBC, owing to a lack of diversity. The Hollywood Foreign Press Association, a group of approximately 90 journalists that make up the Golden Globes jury, quickly announced a 50% increase in their staff with the explicit intention of recruiting black journalists. A similar case is that of the Grammy Awards organisation, which, in 2021, faced accusations of racial bias for nominating too many white artists! White singer Alastair Moock thus decided to withdraw from the competition, which was a spectacular sign of virtue, stating that 'after this year, to have an all-white slate of nominees seemed really tone-deaf'.

Building on an already well-established anti-racist foundation, the concept of white privilege and the rhetoric that goes hand in hand with it have, in the space of a mere few years, led to the favouring of racial minorities in every conceivable way. It is no longer a question of skill or merit. Instead, it is now imperative to reward, recruit or fund diversity at the expense of Europeans, under any and all circumstances. This socio-moral injunction is ultimately justified only by the very existence of whites, stigmatised as they are by an inalienable oppressor status that legitimises such deprivation.

Concessions, compromises, and reparations will not be enough to satisfy an ideology that always demands more. Whether political or racial, the communities brought together by their systematic criticism of the West and its values want neither fairness nor equality. What they strive for instead is power. Beyond the status to be acquired, the money to be earned, and the positions to be claimed lies *the space* to be occupied. White leftists are the useful idiots of such conquering minorities. The strategy is an obvious one: In the aftermath of the reparations, only domination and subsequent replacement can follow.

RACIALISED PRIVILEGES

WHO DOMINATES who?

In the victimhood race, Africans are ahead of everyone else. As for Muslims, they enjoy great advantages thanks to the following: the concept of Islamophobia, which is equated with racism; white people's alleged misunderstanding of Islam, ever perceived as a type of Christianity for Arabs; and the clever propaganda that allows Muslim populations to be presented as oppressed when, in actual fact, they are often the aggressors, as seen with the Palestinians, Rohingya, Uyghurs, etc. Colonisation and especially slavery, however, are what competes with other historical memory narratives and is brandished in our faces as the most heinous historical crime. Having been subjected to this more than others, Africans now particularly benefit from this victimhood status. Those that criticise white privilege and supremacy clearly explain that racism and discrimination are the modern extension of slavery, which remains both structural and ever budding.

Moreover, black people can readily partner up with Muslim victimhood, uniting themselves with such struggles and reinforcing their own image. Since black people are said to be the most victimised, they have the opportunity to support all struggles as part of a general logic of Third-Worldism and global white oppression. It is indeed more difficult for Muslims to be held responsible for anti-black racism. An African can therefore legitimately support Palestine against Israel by alleging a type of Afro-Muslim victimhood.

Conversely, a North African can only take second place when it comes to decrying slavery, which, incidentally, is still widely practiced in the Arabian Peninsula.

Black people have, furthermore, become the embodiment of what is most different from white people. As previously seen with advertising, they allow for the inclusion of all minorities. To highlight a black person on television, in music, or in advertisements is to represent all other non-White people through them. Admiring black people is the best way to avoid being racist and demonstrate one's love for all differences and diversity (including the sexual kind). To pity them is to pity all victims through them. Africans thus embody the entire spectrum of intersectionality.

Muslims, for their part, can only claim to be victims of Islamophobia in Europe. This argument, however, is undermined by the evidence of the civilisational conflict between the West and the Islamic world, which is manifested particularly through political-religious demands and a growing number of attacks. In comparison, black people seem less aggressive in their demands.

What is African is also the embodiment of archetypal Otherness. Thanks to the strong impact of the American entertainment industry, which is dominated by African-American values, every African is now seen as endowed with a positive identity that has become a sort of role model. This status has been erected alongside the constant demonisation of whites, as well as that of European civilisation and its history. Rap, sports and their respective African stars are now the main vectors for the representation of Western youth.

In language, behaviour, tastes, and style, the black man has become the new cultural reference. He is symbolically dominant, at times even overwhelmingly so. His position is reinforced by mass immigration, which favours the reverse assimilation of young Europeans, who, mentally speaking, are being increasingly Africanised. The cultural and symbolic place of the black man in the West obliterates what is inappropriately termed 'white privilege', that is, our plain and simple normality, the very norm epitomised by the social codes implemented by the indigenous peoples of European descent on their own soil.

Whether it's intellectual discourse, media propaganda, the social pressure exerted on white youths, or political activism, everything is now converging to impose new cultural benchmarks that are to replace the European values and social codes that previously prevailed. We are not talking about balance or equity here. According to anthropologist Wiktor Stoczkowski, who also acts as a researcher at the Collège de France, 'the objective of de-colonial studies is clearly formulated by its own leaders: it is all about reversing the very relations of domination [...] and imposing a new cultural, ideological, and moral hegemony on the whole of French society'.

This profound alteration is compounded not only by rhetorical and social hostility, as detailed in the previous chapters, but also by physical animosity: in some neighbourhoods, Europeans are no longer welcome on their own soil. Increasingly alienated and dominated in their own countries, guilt-ridden whites must give way to others. Indeed, they are already fleeing the suburbs and, at times, even leaving entire cities now taken over by new, conquering populations that are to replace them. These populations refuse to adopt the social and historical codes of local people and strive to impose their own through a colonisation that is taking place on an unprecedented scale and at unparalleled speed. White 'privilege' is thus synonymous with not having the right to complain about the replacement of one's culture or the dispossession of one's ancestral land.

Paraphrasing Marx, Raymond Aron[1] once stated that 'although men do make history, they have no knowledge of the history they make'. Whether it's a matter of wilful intent among activists or merely the collective unconscious of the masses, the ongoing process is clearly one of revenge. It is now non-whites, and particularly Africans, that are colonising the civilisational space of whites. Formerly colonised populations have now become colonisers,

1   TN: A philosopher, sociologist, political scientist, historian and journalist, Raymond Aron was one of France's most prominent 20th-century thinkers.

primarily on a demographic level, but also through a mixture of demoralisation, social asphyxiation, and guerrilla warfare rooted in 'gratuitous' attacks and savagery. The mental, aesthetic, and even territorial universe of Europeans is becoming increasingly alien to them. Whites and their norms are no longer dominant, whatever de-colonialists may claim.

This domination is such that, beyond its mental and moral dimension, it is now more pervasive than any hypothetical white privilege ever was in our contemporary West. Long before the end of South African apartheid, racial minorities were considered precisely that in both Europe and the West: minorities, not inferior popula-tions. They were not singled out everywhere, whether in advertising or in films. At worst, they were mocked through various stereotypes, just as blondes, Cabu's *Beauf*,[2] and, of course, white men still are today.

Afro-Muslim Privilege

The above-mentioned allegation can even be reversed, with Afro-Muslims actually benefiting from genuine racialised privilege that comprises all the previously detailed advantages: victimhood, af-firmative action, the status of a new cultural reference, and so on. This privilege also manifests itself through the existence of lawless, no-go areas where the police no longer dare to enter, at a time when white people are fined for not having a Covid-19 certificate. The oc-cupation of our streets, where a white woman can readily be labelled a slut simply because she is wearing a skirt (but never when she is covered or veiled) and where a white man can be killed for looking at someone the wrong way or on account of a refused cigarette, is also a manifestation of Afro-Muslim privilege.

Another is the recurring mobilisation of a section of the show business world in support of immigrant offenders such as Adama

---

2   TN: According to dictionaries, a *Beauf* is a specific type of redneck depicted by Cabu, a French cartoonist, and often defined as a rude, uncultivated and narrow-minded person.

Traoré, while white people like Axelle Dorier, Mélanie Lemée, and Philippe Monguillot are slaughtered amidst the total indifference of our stars. Then there is also the right to be considered a martyr, as seen with George Floyd and Brahim Bouarram. The latter died in 1995 and remains the only case where an Arab was killed in France by the 'far right' — which is why the left brings him up systematically. None of the white people killed by scum are ever mourned. All are forgotten within a couple of days, if the media even deign to talk about them at all.

Racialised privilege is when one asserts that everything is racist except anti-white racism. Perhaps we should say this to the children who are the only white pupils in their class; to the Europeans who live in 'sensitive neighbourhoods'; to those who, on a daily basis, are insulted or attacked by the proponents of 'diversity'; and to the white farmers of South Africa. All it takes is for right-wing whites to sign an open letter or take a photo of themselves in blue down jackets[3] in front of a symbolic border to be denounced as violent and dissident. Scum, on the other hand, can be defended politically even when they burn down police stations. Ever a privilege enjoyed by racialised people, defending them is always within the bounds of what is socially acceptable, regardless of context. There is always an excuse for their behaviour, even in the case of the Kouachi brothers,[4] whose 'miserable childhood' was chronicled by Médiapart.

Afro-Muslim privilege implies lenient treatment at the hands of the justice system, a systematic presumption of innocence for scum, and targeting our law enforcement units with opprobrium at the slightest accusation. What we are now witnessing is thus more a matter of systemic laxity than systemic racism. The media typically alter the first names of offenders to avoid stigmatising certain populations, or invoke the 'no generalising' principle after each and every

---

3   TN: An item of clothing often worn by members of the *Génération Identitaire* [Identitarian Generation] movement.

4   TN: The two men responsible for the Charlie Hebdo massacre.

Islamist attack. At the same time, they do not think twice about openly revealing the identity of European criminals while denouncing white supremacy in connection with attacks committed by lone wolves such as Anders Breivik or Brenton Tarrant.

Being able to choose the reason for one's outrage is also an Afro-Muslim privilege. After 150 years since the abolition of slavery in most Western countries, all white people are still deemed guilty and expected to repent, even though the vast majority of their ancestors never actually owned or sold slaves. And yet, no one talks about the slavery still practiced in several African countries, Haiti, or the Gulf States.

No one ever asks Muslims to assume responsibility for the persecution that the Yazidis, Copts, Kurds, Kalash, and so many others still face in Muslim countries. The slightest insult hurled by a white person at a black person unleashes passions, while no one ever speaks of the countless attacks in the opposite direction. Choosing to specifically blame white people through her 2001 memory law, Christiane Taubira would admit, in 2006, that she wanted to avoid mentioning the Arab-Muslim slave trade so that 'young Arabs would not have to bear the full weight of the legacy of Arab wrongdoings'.

Racialised privilege also means benefiting from the benevolence of the academic caste. In the words of American essayist David Horowitz, 'Black studies celebrates Blackness, Chicano studies celebrates Chicanos, women's studies celebrates women, and whiteness studies attacks white people as evil.' White people are thus the only ones without an academic field that either praises them for who they are or complains about their plight. Critics of white privilege will surely object to this and claim that all other disciplines are Eurocentric and, therefore, white people don't need to be valorised. At the same time, however, they want to deconstruct every single one of them, so what will Europeans be left with then?

Additionally, Afro-Muslim privilege is synonymous with being able to whine about cultural appropriation whenever a white person dresses up as a member of the Sioux or sports dreadlocks, but finding it perfectly normal for an Arab to wear a three-piece suit, for an African woman to straighten her hair, or for ballet to forcibly become multiracial. It also has people applaud when Arsène Lupin and Queen Anne Boleyn are played by black actors, while feeling offended by the idea that Rosa Parks or Nelson Mandela could be played by non-blacks. In the case of black people, it is to systematically display the highest possible level of racial pride and self-esteem (an attitude that is alleged to unmistakably result from oppression) in various surveys on the subject, whereas whites always have the lowest.

It's all about the humour-related taboo of mocking black people or Islam while white people can be readily humiliated. It's about others holding racialised meetings in single-sex settings, but prohibiting white people from organising such gatherings themselves. It's about having the right to embrace one's roots and culture and being proud of them, at a time when the native French are told, on a daily basis, that their country is the product of immigration and that they are to 'creolise' themselves, as stated by Jean-Luc Mélenchon,[5] while even Emmanuel Macron declares that 'French culture does not exist'.

Afro-Muslim privilege also implies the opportunity to enjoy the standard and lifestyle of Western societies despite the considerable cost,[6] resulting in a veritable bottomless pit. In February 2021, Emmanuel Macron stated that 'more than 10 million of our fellow citizens have families on the other side of the Mediterranean'. Despite not being particularly famous for being alarmist with regard to the migration situation, the National Institute of Statistics and Economic Studies (INSEE) estimated, in 2018, that there were a total of 8.657 million immigrants or direct descendants of non-European immigrants in France, totalling 13% of the population. This

---

5   TN: Born in August 1951, Jean-Luc Antoine Pierre Mélenchon is a French politician who has been the de facto leader of the *La France Insoumise (LFI)* political party since its founding in 2016. The party is very left-oriented and has sought cooperation with the French Communist Party (among others).

6   TN: A reference to the various social benefits immigrants receive.

is obviously without counting their third and fourth generations once the first has been naturalised.

This immigration costs infinitely more than it generates. Jean-Paul Gourévitch, an academic specialist on the issue, estimates an annual deficit of €20 to €25 billion. According to the Centre for Prospective Studies and International Information, an institute that falls under the authority of our Prime Minister, immigration cost up to 1.64% of our GDP in 2011 when one included the second generation. This represents a sum of €40 billion per year.

These calculations are made without taking into account naturalised French citizens, who, on paper, are considered French. Acquiring the French nationality does not, however, magically transform them into fully integrated citizens or significantly contributing taxpayers. According to the INSEE, French people with no ties to immigration had an unemployment rate of 7.7% in 2018, whereas French people of immigrant descent had a rate of 13.3%, which is almost double. Submitted to Emmanuel Macron in June 2021, the Blanchard-Tirole report notes that '*activity rates among non-European immigrant women are particularly low. More than 45% of them are unemployed or not looking for work*'. Considering the net annual cost of immigration, the much higher unemployment rate among non-Europeans, and the fact that immigration drives down wages, it is easy to conclude that non-European immigration to France results in a colossal net loss for our population of European origin.

In addition to these calculations, there are also direct costs. To give just one example, the toll of our urban policy and suburban plans amounts to 'at least 200 billion' according to *Contribuables Associés*[7], that is billions which were simply swallowed up by the suburbs at the expense of our native French population. In 2006, the research director at the CNRS,[8] Dominique Lorrain, drew a comparison between the deprived neighbourhood of Hautes-Noues, in

---

7   TN: *Contribuables Associés* [Associated Taxpayers] is a French taxpayer association and lobby.

8   TN: The French National Centre for Scientific Research.

Val-de-Marne, and the Cité Verte neighbourhood in Verdun. While the social characteristics of these two areas are extremely similar, with the notable difference being a much higher proportion of foreigners in Hautes-Noues, he established that the latter benefited from a public investment of €12,230 per inhabitant through urban policy, while Verdun only received an amount of €11.8 per inhabitant! That's literally a thousand times less.

More generally, the suburbs, including those labelled 'sensitive', benefit from all the advantages offered by the large city that they are attached to: frequent and efficient public transport, an extremely dynamic job market even for people with few or no qualifications, comprehensive public services, cultural and sports facilities, higher education establishments, social housing taken over by immigrants, etc. The buildings are renovated as part of the city's policy, and the associations are generously supported by the public authorities.

Peripheral France, i.e. the France of small towns and rural areas, has nothing of the sort: residents are still dependent on their cars even for the slightest journey, while factory relocations condemn entire departments to economic death, cinemas and libraries remain rare, public services are non-existent, and bistros, medical practices and bakeries end up closing one by one... And to enable their children to study, families must be able to afford the costs of housing in a major city. This situation has lead Dominique Lorrain to state that '*if one regards equality among citizens of the same nation as being defined by material access to public assets, then the inhabitants of Meuse (and the same reasoning can be applied to many other departments) are being discriminated against*'.

The list of net costs would be too long to compile. As early as 2002, Nobel Prize winner Maurice Allais declared that an immigrant's infrastructure costs — including housing, roads, hospitals, schools, workplaces, etc. — were four times higher than his or her contributions. Moreover, these already edifying figures should not obscure the fact that a large portion of the costs incurred by non-Europeans remains incalculable — daily degradation or damage resulting from riots, schooling, illegal employment, social security fraud, economic benefits enjoyed by our naturalised citizens, increased security measures, justice, prisons, healthcare, etc. Such economic burdens are borne by our taxpayers, who, as suggested by demographic research, are still overwhelmingly white. Wealth transfers are thus a one-way street.

France does not allow ethnicity-based statistics. However, it would be difficult to deny that our exorbitant expenses are indeed due to the presence of Afro-Muslims. A few simple examples enable us to infer this: the high concentration of immigrants in suburbs lavished with subsidies, the higher birth rate of non-European women who receive the corresponding child benefits, and the higher crime rate characterising these populations. According to Fabienne Klein-Donati, a public prosecutor at the Bobigny High Court, Seine-Saint-Denis is 'the most crime-ridden department in France' with 84.73 crimes and misdemeanours per thousand inhabitants. Consider also the city of Detroit, Michigan: it was 90% white in 1940, then 78% black in 2019, and it now holds the unfortunate record of the highest violent crime rate in the United States for cities with over 100,000 inhabitants.

Poverty is no excuse for this. The department of Creuse, which has the fourth lowest median income per capita in France, also has the second lowest crime rate. In 2001, Sébastian Roché, a sociologist and professor at the IEP[9] in Grenoble, demonstrated in a CNRS-funded study that, at the same social level, young people of North African origin are significantly more delinquent than young people of French descent. They are even twice as likely to commit crimes.

What is true for France can hardly be different for the rest of the white world. Population change leads to the Third-Worldisation of the West. To maintain social peace, leaders pay what it takes — with the money of our natives. This is apparently also white privilege: paying for a less productive, more crime-prone, and largely

---

9   TN: The Institute of Political Studies.

unassimilated population that Europeans do not want. And yet, it would seem that not all non-whites are a burden.

Asian Privilege?

Even when one puts aside the obvious political exploitation and the circular reasoning that structures it, the discourse held on white privilege faces a major issue, namely the fact that Asian privilege could be another racialised privilege. The highly varied Asian ethnicities seem to have no difficulty in succeeding both economically and socially, whether in their countries of origin or in the West.

Asia, however, was also colonised by whites. Hong Kong was a British colony from 1842 to 1997 and was brutally occupied by the Japanese for four years during World War II. Yet, the island is one of the most developed regions in the world, with the tenth highest GDP per capita in terms of purchasing power parity and the fourth highest human development index. And what about Taiwan, which was successively under Dutch, Spanish, Chinese, Japanese, and then again Chinese rule between 1624 and 1949? Although the island's history is a tumultuous one, it is nonetheless rich, politically stable, and indispensable to global economy.

All in all, Europeans had Asian colonies for nearly five hundred years. Most of Asia and Oceania were, at one time or another, sometimes even for long periods, under Western domination (the history of Dutch Indonesia, which practiced the slave trade, spans across more than four centuries). And still, almost all modern Asian states are doing better than African ones, even though the latter continue to receive substantial financial aid from the West.

The best counter-example is that of Ethiopia, which was never colonised by whites. At most, the country was politically occupied by Mussolini's Italy for a period of five years, although Italy never truly controlled more than 10% of the territory. What this occupation left behind were thousands of kilometres of roads, 25 hospitals, and many schools. According to the International Monetary Fund, however,

Ethiopia still ranks 158th in the world (out of 188 countries) in terms of GDP per capita and purchasing power parity. To quote Bernard Lugan, 'there are 40 African countries, from a total of 52, that still live on nothing but international charity'.

In addition to doing better in their own homelands despite colonisation, Asians tend to outperform other immigrants in Western countries. According to the denouncers of white privilege, white supremacy allegedly fuels differences between various immigrant populations to prevent them from uniting, thus enabling whites to remain above the fray. The problem is that, in the case of Asians, they often do better than whites themselves. If white privilege were a system that structures Western societies and is rooted in racism and colonial history, why would specific categories of immigrants prosper so much? There are, in fact, many aspects to this success.

According to the U.S. Department of Commerce, the average annual income of African Americans was $43,862 in 2018, compared to $65,902 for whites and $87,243 for Asians. Generally speaking, Indians are the highest-earning group on average, with $135,702 per year, far ahead of the top-earning whites, namely Australians, who only earn $100,856.

At the end of their school education, many Americans wishing to enter university take a standardised written test called the SAT, which assesses their skills in writing, critical reading, and mathematics. According to the Department of Education, on a scale ranging from 400 to 1600 points, the average score for black students in 2018 was 946, with white students scoring 1123 and Asian students 1223. The SAT is comparable to IQ tests, which are also standardised. Those who criticise the concept of IQ believe, among other things, that these tests were developed in accordance with European standards. The resulting IQ differences are, however, similar: the average score obtained by Africans living in the West is 85, that of Europeans 100 and that of Northeast Asians 105. It would be difficult to claim that the tests are calibrated to suit white standards and culture when Asians actually perform better than everyone else...

In 2008, still in the United States, 58.9% of Asians were found to have at least a bachelor's degree, with only 41.9% of whites and 28.7% of blacks having attained such a level of education. Even without earning a degree, 78% of Asians, 70% of whites, and 62% of blacks enrolled at university. In France, according to figures provided by the INSEE in 2008, 31% of the children of Asian immigrants had obtained a higher education degree, compared to 25% of native French people, 12% of Algerians, and 15% of Africans, despite the fact that all individuals in France received the same primary school education.

Academic backgrounds are also revealing, as Asians are overrepresented in hard sciences (STEM: science, technology, engineering, and mathematics), while black Americans are overrepresented in public administration and social work. In 2019, the United States tied for first place with China at the International Mathematical Olympiad. The American team consisted of five Asians and one white person. The academic success of Asians is such that many American universities discriminate against them: while, as previously highlighted, blacks benefit from affirmative action and bonus points, Asians face a penalty that may prevent them from entering. Asian Americans are increasingly protesting against this unjust treatment, as it undermines meritocracy.

Another symbol of their successful integration is that the crime rate of Asians is, on average, lower than that of whites. To give just one example, FBI statistics indicate that, in 2018, whites — including Hispanics and Latinos — represented roughly 79% of the population and were responsible for 41.1% of homicides. During the same year, African Americans committed 55.9% of all murders. Comparing this rate to their share of the U.S. population, which totals a mere 13%, one can readily see that they kill about eight times more often than whites, including Hispanics. If the FBI provided more details, we would see that the reality is certainly much worse than that: according to political scientist Charles Murray, who addresses this issue in his book *Facing Reality: Two Truths about Race in America*, Hispanics are arrested five times more often for murder than whites, and blacks 20 times more! By contrast, Asians were found guilty of less than 3% of all murders, even though they represent about 5.9% of the population.

Living standards cannot account for the situation, either: indeed, black and Hispanic communities experience roughly similar levels of poverty. In their 1985 book entitled *Crime and Human Nature*, James Q. Wilson and Richard Herrnstein reported that in the 1960s, Chinatown was the poorest neighbourhood in San Francisco, with the lowest level of education and the highest unemployment rate. Despite this fact, only five Asians were arrested and sentenced to prison in the entire state of California in 1965. A major study published in 2021 by the International Journal of Epidemiology and conducted by Finnish researchers on more than 650,000 of their compatriots confirms that there is '*no causal relationship between childhood family income and subsequent psychiatric disorders, substance abuse, and arrests for violent crimes*'.

Despite colonisation, and in spite of the fact that they are non-native, Asians, regardless of ethnicity, are considered well-integrated, discreet, and hardworking in all Western societies. They achieve wide-ranging success, often more so than white natives. How strange our white privilege is, when it doesn't even favour Europeans under all circumstances! Why doesn't it oppress Asians as well, then? Does white supremacy tolerate the success of some non-whites while keeping others under its yoke? Do Asians have some predisposition to whiteness?

The answer is a more obvious one: there is neither white privilege nor systemic racism pervading the West. There are only degrees of adequacy to peaceful societies founded by peoples with high IQs. The members of some populations simply find it easier to live therein than others.

VIII

A PERFECTLY LEGITIMATE WHITE HERITAGE

Myths of Exploitation

A MORAL AND financial tribute paid to people of colour is demanded both in the name of supposed current discrimination and as a result of the past. Not only did slavery and colonisation oppress and ruin the lives of Afro-Muslims, but Europeans are also accused of having built their success on the backs of others. White privilege has supposedly been erected on the suffering of other peoples. Africa, in particular, is said to have allowed whites to enrich themselves and establish their current dominant position, to the point that white wealth allegedly stems from some ill-gotten gains. This preconceived idea is fuelled by three major myths.

The first, which is specifically French, is twofold: in addition to having fought in a white war in 1914–1918, Afro-Maghrebians supposedly liberated France in 1945, going as far as to rebuild it! Repeatedly mentioned to bestow various virtues upon those people while portraying Europeans as weak, this idea of African blood spilled for France is still resorted to today to justify mass immigration. To some extent, white privilege is said to only survive in France thanks to the aid provided by latter's colonies and is thus all the more unjust.

Regarding World War I, black soldiers of French colonial origin totalled, according to historian Jean-Yves Le Naour, 180,000 out of 8.4 million mobilised French combatants. 135,000 fought on European soil and 30,000 died in combat. Known for his left-wing and pro-Algerian commitment, Benjamin Stora estimates that '25,000 [Algerian] Muslim soldiers perished in that war'. These were, of course, honourable sacrifices, but still only a drop in the ocean compared to the carnage experienced by the *poilus*,[1] of whom 1.4 million died. Some historians even mention 2 million French casualties, not including colonial soldiers. The proportion of colonials killed was not particularly remarkable, either: far from being cannon fodder, blacks and North Africans died in the same numbers as whites, at around 15% of those mobilised.

As for the liberation of France in 1945, the colonial contribution, while undeniable, must be put into perspective. The main effort came from the Normandy landings on D-Day, with 160,000 men that were mainly members of the British, American — including less than 2,000 African Americans — and Canadian armies. While not entirely symbolic in significance, the landings in Provence, which took place a month later, occurred on a smaller scale and were less strategically important. Moreover, French troops were far from being composed exclusively of Afro-Maghrebians, as 40% of the soldiers were of European origin. The most famous feat of arms accomplished by the Maghrebian *Goumiers*[2] remains the *marocchinate* ('Moroccan deeds') after the Battle of Monte Cassino: a series of rapes, pillages, and mass murders of which Italy still retains a most sinister memory. They thus echo the numerous rapes committed in Normandy by black GIs.

---

1   TN: The term *poilus* (hairy ones) refers to the appearance of typical French infantrymen, who had long hair and beards/moustaches.

2   TN: The *Gourniers*, or Moroccan *Goumiers*, were initially tribal irregulars and later regular troops from Morocco that served with the French army during their occupation of Morocco, as well as in World War II and the First Indochina War.

Concerning the alleged reconstruction of France through immigration, it is simply a delusion. According to Daniel Lefeuvre,[3] who assesses the situation in his book *Pour en finir avec la repentance coloniale*,[4] North Africans represented less than 1% of the metropolitan workforce in 1951, the year considered by historians to mark the end of reconstruction. It is therefore clear that France needed Africa neither for its survival, nor for its liberation, nor even for its reconstruction.

The second myth applies more broadly to Western Europe: colonisation is alleged to have largely been to the advantage of Europeans, who derived from it the necessary resources to achieve world domination. In reality, however, it cost the colonisers a great deal of money and greatly benefited the colonised. The purpose here is not to glorify colonisation, but simply to emphasise the fact that it also had many benefits.

Africanist Bernard Lugan points out that '*colonisation was nothing but a brief interlude in the long history of Africa. Until the 1880s, with the exception of Algeria, the Cape of Good Hope and a few coastal trading posts, Europeans had, in fact, kept away from the African continent*'. He then goes on to add that '*France even exhausted itself by building there 50,000 km of paved roads, 215,000 km of all-season tracks, 18,000 km of railways, 63 well-equipped ports, 196 airfields, 2,000 well-equipped dispensaries, 600 maternity wards, and 220 hospitals in which both care and medicines were provided free of charge*'. To give a specific example, Lugan notes that in 1959, Algeria represented 20% of the total budget allocated by the French state.

On a different note, with the exception of Moroccan phosphates, Tonkin coal mines, and a few sector-specific productions, the Empire did not supply France with any rare resources. Our imports from the colonies were even negligible: in 1913, 0.1% of the cotton, 3.2% of the

3   TN: Daniel Lefeuvre was a French historian and a specialist in the colonial sphere.

4   TN: Putting an End to Colonial Repentance.

wool, and 0.2% of the silk imported by France came from the colonies. Coal, vital to the French economy until the 1950s, was not produced by the colonies, which, with the exception of Indochina, had to import it themselves. Even during World War I, colonial imports remained marginal: of the 170 million tons imported, only 6 came from the colonies. Conversely, colonial products often competed with French ones on the domestic market. After the war, for instance, Algerian wine, which was subsidised and purchased more expensively than the market price, as with almost all colonial products, came into direct competition with the wine produced by winegrowers in the South of France, who were already suffering as a result of an overproduction crisis.

A specialist in economic history, the great historian Jacques Marseille expresses the conviction that '*the colonies accumulated trade deficits with France, the amount of which matches the very size of the credits that the latter had to grant them to simply enable them to balance their accounts. From 1900 to 1971, these credits amounted to just over 50 billion 1914 francs [...], more than three times the total amount of American aid to France from 1945 to 1955*'. He then goes on to state that '*even though colonisation may have enriched certain people [...], it cannot be said to have served the interests of France and the French in the long run. One could even say that the French Empire [...] delayed its own modernisation and ultimately did more harm than good to our continental economy as a whole*'. Jacques Marseille had become interested in this subject when hoping to prove certain Marxist theories on colonisation. His research, however, would lead him to change political sides once and for all.

On the other side of the Channel, historian Niall Ferguson, a specialist in the economic history of the British Empire who taught at Harvard and the London School of Economics, reminds us in a long article published in 2003 that there is a '*historical consensus that the British Empire was economically detrimental*' to the interests of the United Kingdom. He mentions the conclusions of other economists such as Sidney Pollard and Patrick O'Brien, who demonstrated that the capital injected into the colonies had prevented certain investments that would have been useful to the modernisation of British infrastructure and industry. Ever a good liberal, Ferguson still considers colonisation to have ultimately had advantages, since it enabled globalisation, free trade and modern economic growth. The latter, however, are actually the consequences — the benefit of which is debatable — of an entire historical process that is not necessarily linked to the billions which, at the time, were injected into the Empire at the expense of the British.

Similarly, the Dutch economy has never been in better shape than following the decolonisation of Indonesia. According to Dutch historian Henri Wesseling, the '*Dutch economy prospered spectacularly: the increase rate in our national income per capita averaged about 3.5% per year between 1950 and 1970, i.e. seven times higher than in the first forty years of the 20th century [...] Unemployment remained very low almost constantly (with 1.2% in 1957), despite a spectacular increase in population — from ten to thirteen million between 1950 and 1970 — and in spite of the elimination of employment in the "Indian sector"*'.

The funds invested in colonial infrastructure, bridges, hospitals, administrative buildings, and schools using European taxpayers' money are beyond count. Equally immeasurable is the legacy of Western hygiene, medicine, education, and technology left by whites for Africans to enjoy. Essentially financial sinkholes, colonial empires were often, from the perspective of European nations, rather a matter of prestige, geopolitical competition, and commercial relays than a question of profitable resource exploitation. Indeed, not all whites embarked on this adventure with equal enthusiasm: Bismarck, for instance, was delighted at the fact that France and the United Kingdom were exhausting themselves in their colonial adventures while he unified Germany, preparing it both economically and demographically for the war of 1870.

Last but not least, the final myth regarding the very foundation of white supremacy concerns the entire West, since it centres on the slave trade. The latter is generally described as having been extremely lucrative, to the point that some actually believe that it enabled the industrial revolution in Europe. Lugan definitively debunks this tall tale in his reference work entitled *Esclavage: l'histoire à l'endroit*.[5]

He quotes historian David Eltis, who estimated that in the 18th century, at a time when British colonial trade was at its peak, the slave trade constituted less than 1.5% of the English merchant fleet and less than 3% of its tonnage. Eltis argues that *'the slave trade constituted such a small part of the Atlantic trade of the European powers that [...] its contribution to the economic growth of [these] powers would have been insignificant'*. A professor of economic history, David Richardson has also shown that *'the contribution of slave capital to English capital formation rarely exceeded 1% [...] On average, the contribution of the slave trade to English capital formation was around 0.11 % annually.'*

All examples support this interpretation. Guillaume Daudin, a professor of economics at the University of Paris-Dauphine, has demonstrated that the profits resulting from the few French slave traders that actually existed amounted, at best, to 6%, which was far from sufficient to stimulate the entire national economy. As for Olivier Pétré-Grenouilleau, a specialist in the slave trade issue, he has established that Dutch slave traders made an average of only 2.1% in profits between 1730 and 1790. As for the exploitation of slaves, it was far from profitable. Pétré-Grenouilleau has determined that in 1700, the gross product of all British slave colonies barely rivalled that of a small English county.

As summarised by Bernard Lugan, *'if slave trade profits did account for the Industrial Revolution, Portugal would be a great power today, especially since the country embraced decolonisation at a much later point'*. However, Portugal never had its own industrial revolution

---

5   TN: Slavery: History Put Right.

and had, until joining Europe, been rather a Third World country. Furthermore, is it truly necessary to emphasise the fact that the French industrial revolution took place during the second half of the 19th century, following the abolition of slavery, and was confined to the north and east of France, far from its former slave ports of Nantes and Bordeaux?

Likewise, it is often said that the United States was founded on slavery. The reality, however, is quite different. During the Civil War, the slave-owning South was economically more fragile than the abolitionist and industrialised North. The Union won the war less through the valour of its men than through the efficiency of its own production and its overwhelmingly white workers. Slaves, in fact, prevented the Confederacy from rivalling its enemy. Moreover, until World War I, almost all black people still lived in the American South. The northern and western states were, at the time, much more industrialised and economically prosperous. Clearly, these states were not built by slaves or their descendants, since the latter did not even live there. On the contrary, slavery delayed the economic development of the southern states, just as the colonies were a burden to European countries.

The prejudiced and partial approach of blaming whites casts a softening veil over other forms of slavery. In this regard, Pétré-Grenouilleau's estimates of the various slave trades are very telling indeed: the Western slave trade is said to have involved 11 million sub-Saharan Africans, the inter-African slave trade around 14 million, and the Arab-Muslim slave trade nearly 17 million. The latter, brilliantly detailed by Senegalese anthropologist Tidiane N'Diaye in his work titled *Le génocide voilé*,[6] spanned fourteen centuries and was particularly barbaric, with emasculation and castration almost systematic. N'Diaye estimates that there are only 1 million descendants

---

6   TN: The Veiled Genocide.

of black slaves in Muslim countries, compared to nearly 40 million African Americans.

Beginning in the 18th century, Arab-Maghrebians also proceeded to hunt for Africans for the purposes of slavery, something that whites almost never did, contenting themselves with buying slaves from African tribes along the coast. As acknowledged by Beninese artist Romuald Hazoumé regarding the Western slave trade, *'if there had been no seller, there would have been no buyer'*. Former Benin President Mathieu Kérékou would also recognise the *'shameful role played by Africans during the slave trade'*.

The end of such trades was a consequence of colonisation. Moreover, the populations of sub-Saharan Africa were perpetually at war before the arrival of Europeans, as the most powerful ethnic groups attempted to subjugate others, capture slaves and sell them. All civilisations practiced slavery at some point: European civilisation abolished the practice, thus bringing peace to the continent.

Sweat and Blood

Dualistic and mendacious interpretations of history fuel victimhood. Non-whites feel entitled to demand accountability, while whites are led to believe that they owe it to others. It was primarily through their own labour, however, under extremely harsh conditions and despite numerous conflicts, that Europeans achieved the prosperity that they are now being criticised for whenever others claim to denounce white privilege.

Europe also fell prey to invasions and colonisation. For nearly eight centuries, the Iberian Peninsula was completely or partially under harsh Muslim rule. Some historians have attempted to portray this occupation as having been peaceful, but the great Spanish scholar Serafín Fanjul laid this historical lie to rest once and for all with his work *Al-Andalus contra España: La forja del mito*.[7] The Umayyads

---

7   TN: Al-Andalus vs. Spain: The Forging of a Myth.

even gained a foothold in France, dominating Septimania for nearly fifty years during the 8th century. At the other end of Europe, the Ottoman Empire also occupied European lands from 1347 onwards, going so far as to threaten Vienna on two occasions and reigning over parts of the Balkans until 1922. Islam spread from Spain to India only through war and conquest.

For a long time, Muslim countries also practiced white slavery. Snatched away from European shores during raids that took place in the 9th century (one of the reasons behind the start of the Crusades) and from the enslaved populations of the Balkans, white slaves are estimated to have totalled around 1 million people between 1500 and 1800 alone. The Janissary Corps, an elite unit of the Ottoman army that numbered up to 67,000 men in 1699, was primarily composed of whites torn from their families as children and then enslaved and raised to be loyal to the Sultan.

All peoples have at some time attempted to dominate or invade their neighbours. From the age of 'great discoveries' onwards, however, Europeans were simply the most effective in this endeavour, thanks to their technological advances. If Europe was able to conquer the world, it was because it was already richer, technologically more developed, and with a longing for discovery. Although some families did enrich themselves through colonisation and the vile slave trade, white privilege, which is but another name for European civilisational success, was attained exclusively through the work, toil, and genius of Europeans.

Whites waged constant war against each other in a series of conflicts that culminated in what Ernst Nolte[8] and Enzo Traverso[9] called the 'European Civil War', which, from 1914 to 1945, claimed the lives

---

8   TN: Ernst Nolte was a German historian and philosopher whose main focus was on the comparative studies of fascism and communism.

9   TN: Born in 1957, Enzo Traverso is an Italian scholar and the author of many books on critical theory, the Holocaust, Marxism, memory, totalitarianism, revolution, and contemporary historiography.

of approximately 50 million Europeans. They also suffered numerous famines and epidemics, the most famous being the Black Death, which killed between 30% and 50% of all Europeans between 1347 and 1352. Almost all white people are descended from peasants or former labourers who toiled their entire lives in extremely difficult conditions. In Central and Eastern Europe, serfdom was not, in fact, abolished until the second half of the 19th century.

It wasn't until the Industrial Revolution that spectacular economic growth began. The effort required was no less demanding, nor living conditions any less miserable. Emblematic of the harsh daily life of white people at the time were underground miners, portrayed in Zola's work *Germinal*. According to the *Statistique Générale de la France*,[10] children made up 12% of industrial workers in 1840; a minimum age of eight was not introduced until 1841 by a law that also limited night shifts. At the end of the 19th century, the minimum age was still nine in Italy, ten in Denmark, and twelve in Germany, with workdays that could last up to 12 hours, as seen in Belgium.

This is not, however, a matter of engaging in victimhood competition. In parallel to these ordeals and hard work, white people distinguished themselves through their technical genius. Although rudimentary printing was known to Asian and Islamic civilisation, it was Europe that would invent the printing press. And even if China did discover gunpowder in the 9th century, it stuck to fireworks. Having mastered this first chemical explosive, white people eventually invented the nuclear bomb and the International Space Station. The entire modern world — including medicine, energy, chemistry, industry, transportation, and digital technology — is rooted in 'white privilege', that is in the inventiveness and audacity of Europeans.

The history of Europeans is not unblemished, of course. It is no more and no less shameful than that of other peoples. It was white privilege, however, that sent the first man into space and robots to

---

10   TN: General Statistics of France.

Mars. It was white privilege that connected the entire world via the Internet after we had already circumnavigated it by ship. It was white privilege that enabled the first human heart transplant, abolished slavery, and planted its flag in Antarctica and at the top of Mount Everest. This is what some have never managed to do and are jealous of; this is what they now want to tame: the pride and Promethean boldness of Europeans, who made the world as it now is. Who can claim that abolishing this European specificity is truly desirable, while also believing that demanding it could ever be legitimate?

Imagine moving to Japan and starting to criticise the country's history, traditions, and culture; or demanding that its borders be opened to the Third World; or calling all Japanese people that complain about your behaviour 'Japanese supremacists', and saying that they enjoy 'Japanese privilege' acquired in the aftermath of their colonisation of Korea, whose inhabitants they once considered inferior; or implementing censorship laws with the aim of punishing those that criticise you. It immediately seems absurd.

And yet, this is exactly what de-colonial activists have been doing in Western Europe. Anything can be targeted as a symbol of white supremacy. It's simply a matter of criticising all that is perfectly normal in Western countries, all that is the historical product of European civilisation. White privilege is even epitomised by the ease with which white people find hairdressers who know how to take care of their hair. Trivial to the point of ridiculousness, as seen with the rather similar example of band-aid colour mentioned earlier, this argument was used by Rokhaya Diallo on *France Inter* in 2018. According to her, Afro-Muslims suffer from not being able to walk into any hairdressing salon and be assured of finding a 'hairdresser suited to curly and frizzy hair'.

Anti-white activists aside, can anyone be truly surprised or even complain that in a European country, whose population is historically and overwhelmingly white, hairdressers are more trained or accustomed to working with typical European hair? Can anyone imagine the white minority that lives in Gabon complaining about black privilege on the grounds that local hairdressers are more comfortable with African curly hair? As for Asians, most of whom have straight hair, do they also enjoy white privilege when they can easily get their hair done in a European country?

White People's Home

The semantic load of the word 'privilege' facilitates this strategy of pulling out all the stops. In the modern mentality shaped by the Enlightenment, privilege can only be unjustified. What it refers to, particularly in France, whose mindset remains strongly impacted by the Revolution of 1789, is an advantage and an often completely un-justified social position obtained unfairly using physical, political, or symbolic force. In current language, the term 'privilege' designates an inequality that systematically borders on abuse of power. This is why it was deliberately chosen to denounce the supposed domination of whites in Western societies. Semantically, speaking of white privilege instils the idea of a twofold injustice: that of a position that is both advantageous and undeserved.

Somehow, these abuses and injustices seem to justify a heavy-handed, sometimes even violent, response to dispossess and punish the privileged. The countless crimes committed by various com-munist movements are merely the ultimate expressions of how far the struggle for 'equality' can go. To the French, the term 'privilege' remains inextricably linked to the night of 4 August 1789, during which the National Constituent Assembly voted to abolish privileges, thus putting an end to the feudal system of the *Ancien Régime* and its three-order society.

The privileges of the *Ancien Régime*, however, were not solely the prerogative of aristocrats and the clergy. Historically, a mediaeval privilege (from the Latin *privata-lex*) was nothing but a specific law. Private rights were indeed granted to specific groups to the exclu-sion of others, but they were granted due to specific circumstances:

services rendered and rewarded, a status granting both rights and duties, or specific living and working conditions.

After Beauvais defended itself victoriously in 1472 against the siege imposed by Charles the Bold, the Duke of Burgundy, King Louis XI proceeded to thank the inhabitants by granting them privileges. The young Jeanne Laisné distinguished herself during the battle by climbing the ramparts armed with an axe, earning her the nickname Jeanne Hachette.[11] She galvanised the women of the town, who joined the battle and ensured victory. The women of Beauvais were thus celebrated by the king in a commemorative procession in which they were allowed to precede the men. They also all had the right to wear, on their wedding day, adornments that had previously been exclusive to noblewomen.

Another example: following the imposition of new taxes, Louis X introduced a series of provincial charters, beginning in 1315. The first was the Charter to the Normans, which established or confirmed several privileges, including the right for Normans to be judged in Normandy according to Norman custom. Similarly, every professional guild enjoyed protective privileges and could organise itself, decide who had the right to practice the profession, and supervise the quality of its artisans' production. Last but not least, as pointed out by Guillaume Travers[12] in his book *Économie médiévale et société féodale*,[13] the aristocracy was far from all-powerful, since '*a lord did not have the right to sell land granted as tenure to a given family*'. If the feudal system was gradually undermined to the point of leading to genuine abuses, it is precisely because of people's growing disrespect for historical privileges.

The *Ancien Régime* was more of a privilege society than a society organised according to the exclusive interests of lords. Each social

---

11   TN: Hatchet Jeanne.

12   TN: A French author.

13   TN: Mediaeval Economy and Feudal Society.

group (including beggars!), trade, and sometimes even territory benefited from its own privileges. Every privilege had its own social, economic, or historical justification. In this sense, if there is one privilege that does seem unjustified today, it is the mass presence of non-white immigrants in European countries, immigrants that benefit from the advantages offered by these societies and their achievements. What have they done to merit such a status? This privilege could, of course, be granted, provided that they remain a small, perfectly assimilated minority that never seeks to change the societies in which they live. This, however, is no longer the case anywhere except in Eastern Europe.

Indeed, senseless is the belief in potential mass assimilation, a belief that remains the liberals' sole response to the chimerical 'identitarian stranglehold' which they fantasise about in an attempt to challenge it. Believing that they could somehow equate those who seek to destroy European societies with those who want to preserve them, they have nothing to offer but universalism. While indeed conceivable for a handful of individuals immersed in a dominant culture, assimilation is both politically challenged by de-colonialists — who consider it a form of implicit racism and a set of Western values that undermines their original identities — and outdated in the eyes of the masses simply focused on being themselves. Whether a matter of will or apathy, the mass presence of non-whites in the West destroys the ethno-cultural homogeneity of the societies that host them and threatens the very survivability of their host peoples.

The real stranglehold, in fact, is between two types of aporia. On the one hand, there are the de-colonialists, for whom race, i.e. an *Ethnos* without a *Polis*, is sufficient in itself, and who are prepared to destroy, out of sheer resentment, everything that they enjoy within white societies. On the other hand, we have the universalists, whose representations and references are all fundamentally European, but who believe that they can somehow maintain their *Polis* despite the replacement of their *Ethnos*. Incapable of seeing that this universalism is in no way universal, since it is fundamentally Western and Christian, they think of their culture as being abstract and autonomous, surrendering to the delusion that it could survive without the actual people from whom it emanates.

However, as demonstrated by Henri Levavasseur[14], identity, including its biological dimension, is the very foundation of the City. Culture is not a theoretical corpus that can be readily transmitted. It is the unique expression of a given people in a specific environment. Although culture is indeed essential, it can only be founded upon race, which remains primordial and fundamental, and thus an ethno-cultural singularity. Among non-natives, cultural assimilation as a characteristic that trumps racial belonging can only manifest itself on an individual level, as its model is always undermined by plain and simple demographics.

The assimilationist model is, however, no longer conceivable or even desirable. Demographic dynamics threaten the very racial foundation on which European societies and cultures were erected. All political, philosophical, religious, institutional, economic, or even artistic considerations, including antagonistic ones, are emanations of a particular ethno-genesis. The rivalries between capitalism and socialism, male/female complementarity and radical feminism, contemporary art and figurative art, or even essentialism and existentialism, are primarily white concerns.

And if there is indeed still a justified privilege in the mediaeval sense, it is certainly the fact that European societies reflect a way of life in which natives are the norm. After all, they are the ones who are at home. White people are the legitimate owners of their own countries and, as such, establish the rules there, ensuring the prevalence of their cultures and that of their own representations. If white privilege does exist, it is, in fact, only the usufruct of the heritage established by their ancestors — what they worked for, fought for, or died for.

---

14   TN: Henri Levavasseur, *Identity: The Foundation of the City - Reconciling Ethnos and Polis*, trans. Roger Adwan (London: Arktos, 2025).

This 'privilege' is thus a white legacy. Nothing is more natural for Europeans than to be themselves on the land where their ancestors are buried and where their morals, customs, and relationship to the world prevail.

Jean Raspail[15] wrote that '*every man and every nation has the sacred duty to preserve their differences and their identity for the sake of their own future and past*'. This is what all the other peoples of the world demand for themselves today. It is, in fact, because peoples differ from one another that they all have the right to a 'home', to their own fatherland. And yet, white people are the only ones to be reviled in this regard; to be systematically made to feel guilty and insulted for embracing their own way of life in their own countries. In his lecture entitled *Race et Culture*,[16] Claude Lévi-Strauss[17] stated that '*one should not feel guilty about placing a way of life above all else and thinking it better than the rest*'. Yet, Europeans are the only ones to be pressured to change, to forget who they are and make way for others.

It is perfectly conceivable for the historical legitimacy of white countries outside Europe to be challenged. That, however, is not the purpose behind the struggle against alleged white privilege, as it targets ethnic Europeans everywhere in the world, both in Europe and elsewhere, in the exact same manner. To give in to white privilege discourse in any given country validates it everywhere else. What is being condemned here is the free existence of white people as such, along with their way of life, their collective being, and their right to identity. To those that long to destroy white heritage, Europe is wherever Europeans live — so the latter had better take note of this.

---

15   TN: Jean Raspail was a French explorer, novelist, and travel writer.

16   TN: Race and Culture.

17   TN: Born in Belgium, Claude Lévi-Strauss was a French anthropologist and ethnologist whose work was decisive in the development of the theories of structuralism and structural anthropology.

Conclusion: 'To exist is to fight that which denies me.'

The concept of white privilege is a weapon. Behind this notion, as well as behind all the theories, demands, and financial or social strategies that accompany it, one can readily make out a constant, looming hatred of white people. More specifically, hatred for the white male, considered a white evil. But white women, including the most feministic and anti-racist ones, should not think themselves immune. Their time will come to be unanimously targeted by diversitarian vindictiveness.

Concealed beneath the trappings of social sciences that operate in isolation and, in most cases, resort to tautological reasoning, this hatred, along with its diverse motivations, is fuelled by a discourse of permanent victimhood. Ever pernicious, it is now gaining ground for various reasons among a growing segment of our youths, the bourgeoisie, and intellectuals. The idea that white people enjoy, both unfairly and unconsciously, structural privileges that are inherent in Western societies heralds a bleak future.

Whether it is actually a false rebellion fully embraced by the political and media elite and by liberalism itself, a progressive religion whose zealots threaten unbelievers, or an ideology weaponised in a desire for geopolitical domination, or even plunder and conquest, the self-fulfilling concept of white privilege adapts to everything and will ultimately justify anything. Hateful of what they cannot become, its most determined supporters seek to punish, subjugate, and expropriate Europeans. And they do not hesitate to resort to social violence. To many, even the slightest suspicion of racism justifies physical violence, thus raising fears of larger-scale happenings already foreshadowed by the attacks against white people in South Africa.

It is pointless to believe that apologies, contrition and negotiation could ever appease those who want to destroy whiteness; indeed, such a cowardly attitude will only serve to galvanise them. Equally absurd is the universalistic response, the hope for a return to a world that is alleged to have preceded the clash of civilisations. Mirroring those who deny the right of white people to exist as themselves, universalists deny the legitimate right of white people to their own human expression: the latter must belong to everyone, even if this were to lead to its dissolution or disappearance. Universalism thus also leads to the destruction of the white world. To confront this double negation, this 'negative' stranglehold that can only lead to the total submission or replacement of Europeans, the latter must return to the natural form of human politics, one that combines *Ethnos* and *Polis*. Such is the definition of ethno-politics, the socio-cultural substratum rooted in biological identity, denying neither and always acknowledging the unique expression of every people as legitimate.

If Europeans were to end up forgetting who they are or becoming a minority on their own soil, it would be illusory to believe that they could continue to impose their lifestyles, their understanding, their issues, their very being-in-the-world. Those who long to 'abolish the white race' and 'destroy the West' in the name of the struggle against white privilege are well-aware of this. This, in fact, is their actual goal, regardless of whether it is conscious or not, of whether they acknowledge it or not. What is under attack is indeed everything that defines the very being of Europeans, their culture, and, beyond that, the anthropological foundations responsible for the very possibility of them having their own culture. Such a desire for deconstruction-destruction is as much part of a mindset of jealousy and racial hatred as it is inherent in the old revolutionary project of 'wiping the past's slate clean' so as to create a new man, a fluid post-human being stripped of all belonging.

In actual fact, the rhetoric resorted to in the struggle against white privilege doesn't just target the alleged structure. It fuels hatred of white people, both as individuals and as a group. Gradually, what is taking hold is the idea that white people are privileged simply because they are white, regardless of context and of what they do or say: every white person is said to benefit from their whiteness. And by merely existing, every white person is guilty of maintaining this privilege, a symbol of white supremacy and the failure of other populations. Whatever its advocates may publicly claim, the project of dismantling whiteness and preventing its re-establishment can only end with the extermination of those that created it, those who unconsciously convey it and perpetuate it simply by being themselves and having children that look like them.

The concept of white privilege can only lead to an all-out war against Europeans, the beginnings of which are already visible. This is why white people's awareness of who they are, of what they must defend, is as essential as it is inevitable. Following the trauma of the two world wars, Europeans longed to escape history, to forget how tragic it was. Shaped and wielded by their adversaries with the explicit aim of harming them, the idea that white privilege exists reminds them that the rest of the world perceives them first and foremost as white. They cannot escape this situation by simply losing themselves in the abstraction of a formless sort of humanist universalism, by becoming undifferentiated, interchangeable atoms without roots or belonging, lost in a vast global market and an endless search for their own self-interest.

Such is the new war that white people must face today, wherever they may live and regardless of whether they like it or not. It is an identity-based war in which they will either have to assert themselves or risk losing everything, because there is no possible common ground, no concession that would ever be sufficient, as their adversaries want to take it all. A European awakening, the only development capable of stemming the great erasure, seems bound to arise from such an existential threat: 'Where danger grows, also grows salvation', Hölderlin[18] once stated.

18   TN: Johann Christian Friedrich Hölderlin was a German poet and philosopher and a prominent figure of German Romanticism.

As highlighted by Carl Schmitt, man knows what he is, because he knows what he is not. It is because war is being waged against Europeans, a war fuelled by hatred of what they fundamentally and essentially are (that is, white), that they will be able to regain the capacity to rise up and defend their civilisational heritage. What the detractors of alleged white privilege long to destroy is a legacy of which Europeans are the custodians; a white heritage shaped as much through the genius of their ancestors as through the latter's suffering and passed down through the continuity of their own self-expression and their very existence on the land of their fathers. It is therefore up to us Europeans to ensure its protection and, in turn, bequeath it to future generations.

L'INSTITUT ILIADE FOR LONG EUROPEAN MEMORY

L'INSTITUT ILIADE for Long European Memory, based in France, was born from an observation. Europe is but a shadow of her former self. Replaced by outsiders, confused by having lost their bearing and their pride, Europeans have abandoned the reins of their common destiny to people other than themselves. Europeans no longer remember. Why? Because amongst the current elite — whether at school, university, or in the media — no one passes down to them the cultural wealth of which they are the inheritors.

Contrary to this moribund current, L'Institut Iliade has given itself the task of participating in the renewal of the cultural grandeur of Europe and in aiding Europeans' reappropriation of their own identity. Facing the Great Erasure of culture, we intend to work for the Great Awakening of European consciousness and to help prepare Europe for a new renaissance — one of identity, freedom, and power.

L'Institut Iliade's calling is threefold:

- To train young men and young women concerned about their history to always build. To make them the avantgarde of the renaissance for which the Institut calls: men and women capable of giving to civic and political action that cultural and metapolitical dimension which is indispensable. Their motto: to put themselves at the service of a community of destiny, which risks disappearing if it is not taken in hand. Armed with a strong culture relating to European traditions and values, they learn to discern that the adventure that awaits them entails risks and self-sacrifice, but also enthusiasm and joy.

- To promote a radical and alternative vision of the world contrary to the dogmas of universalism, egalitarianism, and 'diversity'. Using all available means, the Institut develops concepts and ammunition to understand and fight the modern world.

- To gather together, especially — but not only — in France, those who refuse to submit and who are inspired daily by the Homeric triad as described by Dominique Venner: nature as the base, excellence as the goal, beauty as the horizon.

L'Institut Iliade's originality, especially with the aim of reformulating and updating knowledge, lies in tying together the seriousness of its content with ease of learning for the greater public, the objective being to demonstrate an authentic pedagogy, and to act in complementary or supportive ways with other initiatives having the same goal.

L'Institut Iliade's action takes place across various channels:

- A cadre school of the European Rebirth, which every year brings together trainees from a wide variety of backgrounds and is already seeing citizens from other European countries participate;

- an annual colloquium — made up of academics, politicians, writers, journalists, and association officials from all over Europe — that meets in Paris to discuss strong and challenging themes, such as 'The Aesthetic Universe of Europeans', 'Facing the Migratory Assault', 'Transmit or Disappear', 'Nature as Base — for an Ecology of Place', 'Beyond the Market — Economy at the Service of Peoples';

- the publication of works — designed as beacons to enlighten readers' thoughts and guide them toward the reconquest of their identity — within several collections, made available in the widest array of languages and European countries;

- artistic exhibitions on the fringes of contemporary artistic trends, allowing the public to take a fresh look at art and rooted creation;

- an incubator for ideas, businesses, and associations to support and help the greatest number of projects — with quality and sustainability criteria — across all fields of civil society (culture, commerce, etc.) that seek to impose a rooted vision of the world and an alternative to the current system, while prioritising structures and projects making an impact in real life;

- an active presence on social media, allowing us to reach new audiences (through videos, publications, annual events, and news presentations), centred around a website that functions as much as a resource hub as it does as a platform for exchanges and debate, notably offering an ideal library of more than five hundred works, a European primer, a dictionary of quotations, and turnkey itineraries for visiting and hiking the prominent places of European memory.

Education through history:

L'Institut Iliade endeavours to uphold in every circumstance the richness and singularity of our heritage in order to draw forth the source and the resources of a serene, but determined, affirmation of our identity, both national and European. In line with the thought and deeds of Dominique Venner, the Institut accords in all its activities an essential place to history, both as a matrix of deep meditation on the future as well as a place of the unexpected, where anything is possible.

CONCERNING EUROPE, it seems as though we will be forced to rise up and face immense challenges and fearsome catastrophes even beyond those posed by immigration. These hardships will present the opportunity for both a rebirth and a rediscovery of ourselves. I believe in those qualities that are specific to the European people, qualities currently in a state of dormancy. I believe in our active individuality, our inventiveness, and in the awakening of our energy. This awakening will undoubtedly come. When? I do not know, but I am positive that it will take place.

— DOMINIQUE VENNER, *The Shock of History*
Arktos Media, London, 2015

Follow L'Institut Iliade at
www.institut-iliade.com
linktr.ee/InstitutILIADE

OTHER BOOKS PUBLISHED BY ARKTOS

VIRGINIA ABERNETHY	*Born Abroad*
SRI DHARMA PRAVARTAKA ACHARYA	*The Dharma Manifesto*
JOAKIM ANDERSEN	*Rising from the Ruins*
WINSTON C. BANKS	*Excessive Immigration*
STEPHEN BASKERVILLE	*Who Lost America?*
ALFRED BAEUMLER	*Nietzsche: Philosopher and Politician*
MATT BATTAGLIOLI	*The Consequences of Equality*
ALAIN DE BENOIST	*Beyond Human Rights*
	Carl Schmitt Today
	The Ideology of Sameness
	The Indo-Europeans
	Manifesto for a European Renaissance
	On the Brink of the Abyss
	The Problem of Democracy
	Runes and the Origins of Writing
	View from the Right (vol. 1–3)
ARMAND BERGER	*Tolkien, Europe, and Tradition*
PAWEL BIELAWSKI	*European Apostasy*
ARTHUR MOELLER VAN DEN BRUCK	*Germany's Third Empire*
KERRY BOLTON	*The Perversion of Normality*
	Revolution from Above
	Yockey: A Fascist Odyssey
ISAC BOMAN	*Money Power*
CHARLES WILLIAM DAILEY	*The Serpent Symbol in Tradition*
ANTOINE DRESSE	*Political Realism*
RICARDO DUCHESNE	*Faustian Man in a Multicultural Age*
ALEXANDER DUGIN	*Ethnos and Society*
	Ethnosociology
	Eurasian Mission
	The Fourth Political Theory
	The Great Awakening vs the Great Reset
	Last War of the World-Island
	Politica Aeterna
	Political Platonism
	Putin vs Putin
	The Rise of the Fourth Political Theory
	The Trump Revolution
	Templars of the Proletariat
	The Theory of a Multipolar World
DARIA DUGINA	*A Theory of Europe*
EDWARD DUTTON	*Race Differences in Ethnocentrism*
MARK DYAL	*Hated and Proud*
CLARE ELLIS	*The Blackening of Europe*
KOENRAAD ELST	*Return of the Swastika*
JULIUS EVOLA	*The Bow and the Club*
	Fascism Viewed from the Right
	A Handbook for Right-Wing Youth
	Metaphysics of Power

OTHER BOOKS PUBLISHED BY ARKTOS

	Metaphysics of War
	The Myth of the Blood
	Notes on the Third Reich
	Pagan Imperialism
	Recognitions
	A Traditionalist Confronts Fascism
GUILLAUME FAYE	*Archeofuturism*
	Archeofuturism 2.0
	The Colonisation of Europe
	Convergence of Catastrophes
	Ethnic Apocalypse
	A Global Coup
	Prelude to War
	Sex and Deviance
	Understanding Islam
	Why We Fight
DANIEL S. FORREST	*Suprahumanism*
ANDREW FRASER	*Dissident Dispatches*
	Reinventing Aristocracy in the Age of Woke Capital
	The WASP Question
GÉNÉRATION IDENTITAIRE	*We are Generation Identity*
PETER GOODCHILD	*The Taxi Driver from Baghdad*
	The Western Path
PAUL GOTTFRIED	*War and Democracy*
PETR HAMPL	*Breached Enclosure*
PORUS HOMI HAVEWALA	*The Saga of the Aryan Race*
CONSTANTIN VON HOFFMEISTER	*Esoteric Trumpism*
	MULTIPOLARITY!
RICHARD HOUCK	*Liberalism Unmasked*
A. J. ILLINGWORTH	*Political Justice*
INSTITUT ILIADE	*For a European Awakening*
	Guardians of Heritage
ALEXANDER JACOB	*De Naturae Natura*
JASON REZA JORJANI	*Artemis Unveiled*
	Closer Encounters
	Erosophia
	Faustian Futurist
	Iranian Leviathan
	Lovers of Sophia
	Metapolemos
	Novel Folklore
	Philosophy of the Future
	Prometheism
	Promethean Pirate
	Prometheus and Atlas
	Psychotron
	Uber Man
	World State of Emergency
HENRIK JONASSON	*Sigmund*

OTHER BOOKS PUBLISHED BY ARKTOS

OTHER BOOKS PUBLISHED BY ARKTOS

RAIDO	*A Handbook of Traditional Living* (vol. 1–2)
P R REDDALL	*Towards Awakening*
CLAIRE RAE RANDALL	*The War on Gender*
STEVEN J. ROSEN	*The Agni and the Ecstasy*
	The Jedi in the Lotus
NICHOLAS ROONEY	*Talking to the Wolf*
RICHARD RUDGLEY	*Barbarians*
	Essential Substances
	Wildest Dreams
ERNST VON SALOMON	*It Cannot Be Stormed*
	The Outlaws
WERNER SOMBART	*Traders and Heroes*
PIERO SAN GIORGIO	*Giuseppe*
	Survive the Economic Collapse
	Surviving the Next Catastrophe
SRI SRI RAVI SHANKAR	*Celebrating Silence*
	Know Your Child
	Management Mantras
	Patanjali Yoga Sutras
	Secrets of Relationships
OSWALD SPENGLER	*The Decline of the West*
	Man and Technics
RICHARD STOREY	*The Uniqueness of Western Law*
J. R. SOMMER	*The New Colossus*
TOMISLAV SUNIC	*Against Democracy and Equality*
	Homo Americanus
	Postmortem Report
	Titans are in Town
ASKR SVARTE	*Gods in the Abyss*
HANS-JÜRGEN SYBERBERG	*On the Fortunes and Misfortunes of Art in Post-War Germany*
ABIR TAHA	*Defining Terrorism*
	The Epic of Arya (2nd ed.)
	Nietzsche is Coming God, or the Redemption of the Divine
	Verses of Light
JEAN THIRIART	*Europe: An Empire of 400 Million*
BAL GANGADHAR TILAK	*The Arctic Home in the Vedas*
DOMINIQUE VENNER	*Ernst Jünger: A Different European Destiny*
	For a Positive Critique
	The Shock of History
HANS VOGEL	*How Europe Became American*
MARKUS WILLINGER	*A Europe of Nations*
	Generation Identity
ALEXANDER WOLFHEZE	*Alba Rosa*
	Globus Horribilis
	Rupes Nigra

www.ingramcontent.com/pod-product-compliance
Lightning Source LLC
Chambersburg PA
CBHW022339280326
41934CB00006B/694